THE MEDI

MINDFULNESS, YOGA,

BREATH & BEYOND

BY

JACQUALINE TARA HERRON

CONTENTS

THE MEDITATIVE SOUL

The Meditative Soul is an exploration and meditation into the inner dynamics of living an unchartered life on the intimate path of awakening to the power of consciousness. People say that you teach what you need to learn and this book is the inner story of what I have received through the many practices that lovingly wove their way into my life with transformative significance.

The greatest mystery to me has always been the fact that once certain meditations had been introduced it was as if I had met an old friend who I knew beyond knowing. Many great masters have shared their teachings with me, yet the real teacher has been my own body and being.

This journey consciously began at the age of 21 when I needed to wake up to the fact that my body was not immortal. I was in real physical pain for the first time and I thought I would be crippled for life. This experience struck a chord of overwhelming resonance and appreciation for how we suffer and awoke a new sense of the true vulnerability of my body and the impressionable fragility of my mind. An inquiring respect for what I had always taken for granted arose within me and I began a journey of self-remembrance that took many forms all rooted in ancient laws of awakening and transformation.

I found prayer and healing within these practices, an honoring of the laws of our mortality and the essence of our immortal consciousness. Our connection to all things. These offerings gave me a purpose to be whole; a pathway through which I could directly experience the blessing of our human form and the miracle of conscious awareness.

Your body is the Key. Its seemingly finite form can look into the infinity of the skies just as it did 10,000 years ago. These practices can take you beyond the periphery of your form into the formless nature of your own awareness, beyond time and space where your immortality resides.

This book tells the story of how I experience it. I hope you enjoy it as much as I have enjoyed recalling it and find a familiar friend - yourself, your universe.

IN GRATITUDE

MAY I SEND GRATITUDE to all the Great Beings who have shined a guiding light in this life. Though many more I name the ones whose embodiment of their truth transferred an essence to me, helping to refine the very fabric of my being.

I am deeply grateful to Gia-Fu Feng of Stillpoint Hermitage for his un-denying nature and lucid mind. He showed me the Taoist path of befriending the natural world without fear where we lived deep within the Isobel Forest. With gratitude to Aitkin Roshi of the Diamond Sangha in Hawaii for his masterly grace and non-interfering dharma during the youthful years of my practice.

With gratitude to Rufus Camphausen who awoke in me the recognition of the Goddess as a part of myself and all phenomena. To Sufi Murshid Isa Kadre whose Crazy Wisdom forged me in the flames of courage and independence. To Catalin whose vision, faith and love nurtures my body and soul. To Phil Caylor from The Nyama School, Dr Vasant Ladd,

Purple Flame, Jim Higgins and the manifestation of Evolve Healing Arts.

In appreciation to Anagarika Munindra, Sharon Saltzberg and Jack Kornfield who opened the doors to Vipassana and Metta Meditation practice ripening the fruit of my heart. To my parents whose lives have been great lessons in themselves; the brave voice of my mother Mindu Hornick and the gift of my darling daughter Habibiana. May I extend love and gratitude to all the many beings who have come to practice and serve with me over the years or walked by my side - to all my friends and family - Metta.

THE INVITATION

Cycling over the cobbled bridges of Amsterdam, nothing seems quite the same any more. As I chain my old Dutch bike to the drain-pipe the neighbours across the road wave with gay pride and wide smiles, in the door-way of their exotic bead shop. The smell of coffee fills the Binnen Visser Straat and though already noon the day is just beginning on this easy morning. I had performed as Nuit, the Egyptian goddess of the infinite night sky the evening before with a theatrical band of story-tellers. We recreated the myth of Nuit the Dark Goddess of the infinite night skywho gave birth to Ra the sun god every day. With dramatic costumes, mystic lights and space age music my whole body was painted azure blue and covered with gleaming silver stars which shone and sparkled as I re-enacted this ritual drama in symbolic dance.

Now I breakfast on my favourite toasted fresh rye bread with avocados, lemons and a pot of fragrant coffee. Sitting in the ray of light that angles its way through the open balcony doors, my mind is far away.

The steep indigo blue velvet stair case fills the auditorium with a soft silence. Everywhere people sit in small groups or alone, still and expectant. The people in line before me are waiting to walk down the shinning river of blue carpet to the central arena below that appeared like a still deep pool of lapiz light.

Suddenly it is my turn and someone whispers from behind that I must cry, cry deeply, convincingly and walk way down into the center of the indigo depth. In the distance beneath I see a tall, slow moving man with silver flowing hair and beard in a mystic shroud of soft billowing clouds. Smiling I think how archetypical he appears in his cloak of majestic secrets. Crying is not how I feel, yet a wave of overwhelming emotion pours out from the labyrinths of my belly and I begin to weep, to wail uncontrollably. The sounds echo and reverberate all around, filling the vast space with all my worldly suffering like a trail of past illusions. Above is a domed glass ceiling softly filtering the golden light. There is no-one here but me anymore. When I arrive at the center the wizened mystic opens his cloak, and embracing me whispers, 'You have done well, you will go to America'. An unexpected relief arises within me and a great peace washes through me and I know that I have just accomplished something significant that only he and I understand. I am blessed.

The impression of the dream was so strong I found myself making plans to fly to New York almost immediately. From there I would make my way across the States though I was not sure how. This journey had been calling for a long time and now I was on my way. Sensing huge changes to come my energy moved swiftly through all the bureaucracy of travel; my spirit was already on that other shore.

This was the beginning of a journey that would reveal my natural sense of familiarity with the world and a feeling of being home wherever I found myself. I was 21 and having just lived two dynamic, creative and explorative years in Amsterdam, with extensive journeys through Europe and the Middle East, I yearned for something completely different.

Inspired by the scholars of the ancient mysteries, befriended through the awakening culture all around me, I was introduced to the pantheon of Egyptian Mythology and Sacred Art; Kabbalah and The Tree of Life; Tarot; The I Ching; all kinds of divination; sun and moon astrology; Robert Graves. *The White Goddess*, and a new found spirituality. I was ready to fly - and hover across the vastness of the earth as the lightness of my being began to evolve. Though I wasn't sure how it would happen I knew that I had to go to America. Instinctively I felt that a freedom lay in that great land, and my heart and mind were full of stories of great journeys and teachers who could show me how to liberate my soul.

My whole youth had been spent in search of some greater significance, some symbolic meaning to my existence and I had turned over many stones. Some were heavily burdened with negative matter and some were imbued with great affirming gifts of life. Inspirational people and literature had turned up the volume of my inquiry and I was nourished by the great minds of a growing culture into consciousness that flourished all around me. The voice of Krishnamurti whose spiritual intellect rose above the crowd and who abstained from being put on a pedestal; The supernatural faith of Paramahansa Yogananda's 'Autobiography of a Yogi'; Herman Hesse whose cult fiction influenced a whole generation of literary and poetic souls; Nisargadatta's enlightened 'I am That'', Mahatma Gandhi who truly showed what it was like to be a political leader with a spiritual message; Elizabeth Haich's book 'Initiation' whose ancient ambience reminded me of my own stirring inner dialogue; Dostoyevsky whose relentless vision of the obscure leapt off the pages and dug deep into my social-psychi: Carlos Castaneda who broke the boundaries of the senses and took us on trans-physical adventures, and many other mystic voices such as Huxley, Kafka, Borges, Gurdjieff, Ouspensky and the literary giants Green and Tolkien. I was driven by a powerful force to inquire, to explore and to celebrate life.

As Mahatma Gandhi said *'Life is a series of experiments'*. We do not need to know the exact results of what we do but we need faith and courage to carry them out. This is how we learn and how we keep our minds open to the reality of what our thoughts and actions create. We can live as if we are in a great laboratory of potential, not knowing how life will turn out, yet living it anyway. We all take risks all of the time, though some may be greater risks than others. For me, now, this book is my risk. I have arrived at a time when I need to take stock of all that passed so far and find meaning and purpose to this indefinable mystery of being, of living in this body on this earth. To give my life a voice. A clear-sounding, unashamed, transcendent voice that rises above the fear of not being met, of not being 'understood' and simply say what has been valuable to me. This is my experiment, to open doors that have been shut and polish the windows of my mind so that I do not forget what has mattered to me, what has shaped my heart and consciousness and made me the sum total of who I now am. And who I am not. The people I have loved and how I loved them. The extraordinary places that map the geography of my inner landscape and has served to guide me, body and soul, into this process.

There are stages in life when we want to be ultra-safe and live by the rules and patterns we have come to know, that we can predict. Living with form can nurture deeper changes and transformation that need to happen way beneath the surface of ourselves. In living with a known predicted structure, we can be contained and this gives us a sense of control, of grounded-ness and protection from unknown forces. In this safe environment we can experiment more deeply reducing the risk of outside interference and concentrating in more hidden areas of our inner life. For those of us who find life challenging, perhaps overwhelming on psychological and emotional levels, having a strong adherence to form and structure can help us to feel supported and maintain a more stable and sane outlook on life.

As children we need structure to give us a growing, tangible sense of ourselves and to comprehend the natural physical laws of physics and the universe. This helps us to learn, to play fairly (or unfairly) and achieve set goals. Yet we also need that form to provide openings through which we can be spontaneous and realize our uniqueness and freedom. To learn how to master and experience certain levels of risk based on the knowledge of those natural laws and the grounded sense of ourselves as human beings. Our self-awareness and spatial awareness. The form must also be formless, offering us opportunities to be inspired to touch the source of the form which is the pure energy and consciousness of our own being.

Yoga gives us a perfect form. A form that abides by the physical laws of your body, your structure and the formless dynamic flow of life as it unfolds within you. When I talk about yoga I include in that its many branches and styles, as well as meditation, and most importantly, the mind of yoga which is one of Acceptance and Gratitude.

Yoga was first formulated as a preparation for meditation as it stills and relaxes the body, calms the nervous system and mind, enhancing focus and deepening the breath. The many forms of yoga may attract people from different walks of life yet inevitably have the potential to lead all into an enriched self-awareness. That is its fundamental story. Its ultimate purpose.

Yoga became my bridge, my discipline and guide, over which I have trodden innumerable times, from my wild, formless, risk taking nature to the predictable sanity of my breath, this solid secure body, my honorable vehicle that exists to contain.

The truth of living is not a technique or a concept.
The truth of living is just to live.
Whether you practice yoga or not
you will still be living.

Yoga is not a religion, it is a teaching and teachings
only become real when the concepts and techniques
have dissolved into ourselves and become

who we naturally are.

Truth is not separate from ourselves.
Truth is an inner knowing that is beyond experience.

Teachings are a communication that takes a certain
form, yet it is when this form has disappeared into
our body, bones, flesh and blood and become
formless that something real has happened. Then a
teaching has been completely communicated.

The practice of yoga simply magnifies

the experience of being alive.
Yoga shines a light on the reality of having a body
and a consciousness so that you will notice it,
eventually becoming absorbed into the inner dynamic
of just living - of being.

Whether you are conscious of it or not you will
breathe until you stop breathing.

You will live until you die.

Yoga makes you conscious of this process of living,
so that you consciously become one with the process

Become the one who lives.

THE BODY OF EVIDENCE

In all the ten directions of the universe,
there is only one truth.
When we see clearly, the great teachings are the same.
What can ever be lost? What can be attained?
If we attain something, it was there from the beginning of time.
If we lose something, it is hiding somewhere near us.
Look: this ball in my pocket,
can you see how priceless it is?

> \- Ryokan
> (Zen Buddhist Monk 1758-1831)

When I first woke up to the value of my body I was living in the clear pine clad air of Manitou Springs in Colorado USA. Many friends had taken the caravan trail to the ashrams of the east but I opted for the great western hemisphere, the wild, wild west. I had always been a spiritually motivated wild child and following the inspirational voices of Ram Dass, Yogananda and Krishnamurti I too wanted to explore that land and be present at the many gatherings mysteriously arising there drawing many an awakening soul into their midst.

Landscapes of mind sculpturing, inspirational beauty led me to follow an uncharted path within myself blended with the liberated flavor that flowed out of the cultural dream of a young America. So in the summer of 1978 my journey began.

There are certain people, unique situations that have a remarkable quality about them. A great teacher or teaching is simply someone or something which inspires you, who touches something in you that resonates and grows. I have had the great good fortune to meet some remarkable souls. By naturally being who they were, these people transmitted an essence that altered the very fabric of my being and nourished the calling of my heart. One thing leads to another and it is true to say that the greatest gifts are often very badly packaged.

Arriving at Stillpoint Hermitage in Manitou Springs, I sat for weeks on the veranda in an old rocking chair aligning the 'Garden of the Gods'; a vast national park in the red earth of Colorado where huge megalithic rocks and boulders stood in a silence that breathed consciousness. The view simply held me as my initiation to this great land ceremoniously unfolded. Having come from a street in Amsterdam where my curtains opened to my neighbor opening theirs, I drank long and deep from this emergence of utter power and beauty. I had not realized the great thirst within me for majestic grace and this landscape filled that space. I was gone.

There are a million of the brightest stars within reach of my outstretched hand, in the darkest, widest expanse of sky I have ever seen. The land is completely flat for as far as I can see and then rises into a spectacular curving horizon of raised mesas. My eyes slowly follow along the mountain ridge and I sense they are miles away. Odd silhouettes of desert dwelling plants stand like curious alien beings observing the barren landscape with caution. Cacti and brush look at each other suspiciously in the dead of night as I walk stealthily on the dry bed of thirsty earth. I am in awe of the power of this place; its' broad unhindered darkness, the solid stillness and blanket of silence with pertinent interruptions of sounds I do not know. Sounds that grip my mind to follow them, to heed their call. Calling me to Attention, to listen and inquire. My hearing is acute and intensely vivid. I am so close to the earth I feel the pull of its magnetism; each step marking a new connection as if I am an instrument of a predestined ritual or earth acupuncture; an apprentice of Don Juan like Carlos Castaneda.

I am so close to the stars they are in my hair like a headdress of celestial diamonds; so close to the magic of this atmosphere that I am as if under a spell. The desert has cast a spell over me and I am a willing victim, willing to be part of this magic that second by second changes my vibration, my chemistry. I am transforming, breathing in the potent purity of this mystic night I lose my mind and grow wings that spread out across the scorched expanse, my spirit lifts up and soars. I have been swallowed up by the thirst of the master of this desert and rewarded with wings that have set me free.

Gia-Fu Feng was an extraordinary, lithe hermit somewhere in his 60s when we met. He was one of the original founders of Esalen Institute in Big Sur California, with Fritz Pearls and Abraham Maslow. Gia-Fu arrived in the United States in 1947 from Shanghai to study comparative religion and graduated with an MA from the University of Pennsylvania. His translation of the *Tao Te Ching by Lao Tsu*, with exceptional photography by Jane English, is a delicately refined piece of work reflecting his Taoist spirit that has become an authentic classic. When I met him he had just bought a piece of land in the Isobel Forest in Colorado where a small group of ten of us shared an unusual life.

Gia-Fu embodied a rare spectrum of human qualities. He practiced *Tai-Chi* like a crane in flight and walked for hours every day. Even in thick snow his light footsteps, only covered by soft Chinese shoes, could be seen for miles on the mountain road. Gia-Fu's translations of the *I Ching*, the *Tao Te Ching* and books on *Tai-Chi* shine with a unique authenticity. He was a master of his own philosophy on life and lived it completely. We approached his awesome yet radiant spirit with great respect as one would a sleeping tiger.

Each day we practiced what Gia-Fu called the 'three Bs': the bubbling of the mind (meditation), the babbling of the mouth *(gestalt)* and the blistering of the feet (walking at least 6 miles a day). We began to rest or sleep at about 8 or 9 pm, as the sun goes down early there. Gia-Fu went to his tree-house bed at 7 pm. Each morning we met for meditation at 3 am which flowed into the gestalt session. A fire always blazed in the hearth and I can clearly remember the reflecting flames across Gia-Fu's angular face. With his pointed sage-like beard he might strike his chest and say *'Today I am angry'* or talk about his life as he would begin the gestalt. Gestalt therapy is founded in the teaching of 'open self-expression', where feelings are expressed through your energy and words. The reasoning of gestalt is that this process then prevents the accumulation of negative or harmful thoughts and emotions from potentially generating an unhealthy state of body and mind. We practiced Tai-Chi, walked, grew our own corn and greens, sighted unusual aircraft from a nearby space station and baked in the sun. We all saw flying saucers and other unearthly shapes sailing above the broad expanse of wilderness. As we went to bed so early our last meal was at 4 pm which I discovered really suited my digestion and deepened my sleep.

Gia-Fu told me one day that he saw I was afraid of nature, that I had not befriended the natural world; so we set up a large tent in the middle of the forest, about half a mile from the main area where I slept alone each night. Wild turkey, deer and even bears roamed the forest. Arising each day at 2.30 am I felt a sense of purpose and meaning as I deftly wound my path to the morning meditation.

As scared as I was I began to enjoy the walk through the forest at night and learnt how to see with my feet in the pitch darkness. On full moons I sauntered, when the silvery light draped every edge in an aesthetic glow.

It is a dreamy, heavily hot bee humming afternoon and I am alone in a glade of soft green trees deep in the Isobel forest. The sun above drenches me in the comfort of its penetrating heat. My arms are extending slowly outwards as I turn on axis in a flow of Tai-Chi form, my arms draw back in as I turn very slowly the other way, my arms moving back out. I am totally at peace, at one with my practice. Then Whoosh, my hair stands on end, my breath stops, my arms stay exactly where they are outstretched, one foot just lifted. It is a bear! No, two bears! I am suspended somewhere above my head, my heart pounding loudly, beating a new and ecstatic rhythm I had not heard before. I stay very, very still as the larger bear and I are swept into an orbit of vibrating sensory awareness. We are in each other's physical proximity, each other's space and there is sudden fear, excitement, hesitation and surprise. Yes, it must be a mother and baby bear, an awesome caramel colored mass of robust fur looking directly at me.

She is so close I can see into her sharp black eyes and she is as surprised to see me as I am her. Her nose lifts and sniffs the air about me. I remain motionless, frozen in joyous shock as our energy interacts. I am suspended for what seems endless time and then she simply turns and walks away. Her baby comes close to me and I feel it's hot breath on my skin, curiously, fearlessly discovering me, then turns to follow its' mother. Relieved, my foot touches ground, my arms drop as the raging pulse within me slows down. I am elated.

Gradually the patterns and sounds of my fellow creatures became familiar and for the first time I felt a homogenous solidarity about life in the rawness of the forest. I had always been attracted to a pure way of living and here I actually felt part of the great wilderness.

Life has a way of stopping you in your tracks just when you least expect it. One unbearably hot day whilst we were building log cabins for the winter, I slipped a disc in my spine. I had never experienced such pain as I crawled about on all fours. I cried and fought the agony for many weeks becoming bad tempered and so tense I was unable to eat. I could not believe that my body had let me down so drastically. How could this happen to me? Just when I was having such an important and inspirational time! Feelings of shame at my inability to control my suffering overcame me and I resisted the sympathy and support of others.

I had to go through this alone. Eventually, unable to sit upright or walk they took me back to Manitou Springs to find a cure.

The house in Manitou was large, meditative and clean. Only a few people presently lived there as everyone was in the Isobel Forest with Gia-Fu. My room was light and spacious, with a view of the mountainside and sky. Autumn was turning to winter fast, and radiant golds and reds merged with sunlight onto my bed. I communed each day with an extraordinary lone brown leaf that hung sympathetically by a thread to the bush outside my window all winter.

My spine took three months to heal. Three months of an inner journey that led me to practice yoga. I had never heard of chiropractors at that time and was taken to meet an extraordinary practitioner who laughed at me warmly when I cried and said 'what has happened to my body, I can't walk'. He gently examined and adjusted me and showed me some basic yoga postures. The grace with which he practiced these simple movements was in itself healing to watch and I felt an immediate affinity with the process.

He told me to be aware of every tiny movement and crevice of my body as if the secret of my whole life were hidden there: not to miss a beat; to breathe *into* the pain, focusing my mind with undivided attention; to practice the movements very slowly and accurately.

Everything he taught me felt like a reminder, something I already knew. Most importantly his dynamic positive energy transmitted an essence to me that showed me the intrinsic power of yoga, of prana to heal. In essence he gave me a key, a path that opened the way to my inner life, to a new friendship with myself and the world. A way to experience happiness from the inside out.

I am lying on my back in the snow white light of my Manitou bedroom. My spine is weak, is sensitive and I can only move very, very slowly. I sense it must be very pink within the damaged tissue. No sudden turns, no lifting or bending. No heavy foods or long interactions with others. I am super sensitive through all my senses and need to be alone. I have become newly attuned to the inner trauma that vibrates up and down my spine. I close my eyes and visualize how my spine might look, one vertebra upon the other, the nerves being squeezed on the right side of my lower lumbar. I remember the picture my healer showed me and focus my mind on the place that is most sensitive.

I breathe into that vulnerable area, letting the oxygen and prana flow down into the restriction, circulating fresh blood into this area of damage, of shock. As I move through the slow measured movement, I breathe in to lift my leg up to the point that feels comfortable, then I breathe out as I carefully move that leg across my body to the other side to the point that feels OK. I bring the leg back and inhale. Set it back down to the floor, exhale.

I repeat each move 3 times. My mind is totally absorbed in this exercise, each time the range of my movement becomes a little wider.

I am deeply relaxed. I am conscious. The following of my movement with my breath has reduced the stress, the fear and the pain. I am connected, in control and I am feeling stronger.

This is my first experience of yoga. My healing master has arrived.

It is within this still internal environment that the molecules of your psychological, emotional and physical make up have an opportunity to re-align and restructure themselves according to the quality of consciousness and physical dynamic of the movements. Reflect for a moment upon the speed at which the earth rotates around the sun. You do not physically feel or see the world turning but your senses perceive the shifts in light and darkness and your body responds by adhering to the circadian cycles of night and day, affecting patterns of sleeping and waking. In fact, your whole body is vibrating at such a rate that in order to experience it you need to be very, very still.

The nourishment I required at this time drew on the mineral and vitamin properties of vegetables and plenty of pure mountain water. Seaweeds, leafy green and sodium rich vegetable like zucchini and kale, with occasional calcium and protein rich tofu, earthy carrots and burdock mixed with all kinds of weird American squash formed the ingredients of my daily soup or salad, allowing my blood to de-tox and be replaced by fresh new cells. This light and simple sustenance gave space for all my energy to flow toward purification, regeneration and healing, giving my digestive enzymes a new source of fuel that would burn more easily, leaving very little trace. My elimination efficiently carried away the residue of old matter and toxic waste. The shape of my body changed and I felt light like the wind and flexible in the very deepest recesses of my muscles, viscera, tissue and bone. A direct sense of my formless origins grew into an inner peace of natural composure that further attuned me to the sensibility of the vibrations and sensations that yoga inwardly creates. Here I discovered the spiritual power of fasting, abstaining from food, which I have drawn on time and again throughout my life to cleanse and regenerate all the internal organs, refreshing the mind and soul.

The snow fell in cascades outside my mountain retreat and I began a diary that was to last for many years. The awareness of my vulnerability and impermanence revealed the sacredness of every day, of every moment. Yoga filled my body, mind and soul with softness and stillness as the healing process unfolded. The awakening I had at that time gave me a sense of gratitude for all that had ever happened to me and most profoundly, for this healing body.

My teenage years had been somewhat toxic and reckless. The realization of just how much physical and emotional damage I had already accumulated began to dawn on me. Through the intensity of the work with Gia-Fu I had dissolved so much of the excess baggage in my body that my form had actually crumpled for a while to make space for the molecules to rearrange themselves on a deeper, more supportive level. I needed that injury. It was a great blessing and profound teaching, an enforced retreat into the sensitivity of the life within me. An opportunity to experience the transformative teachings of physical suffering and reflect in the grace of secret solitude. The experiences with Gia-Fu had prepared my mind and heart to understand and embrace the practice of yoga. There were three things I discovered were essential to me during those months; space, light and solitude.

The softest thing in the universe
Overcomes the hardest thing in the universe.
That without substance can enter where there is no room.
Teaching without words and work without doing
Are understood by very few.

-By Lao Tsu ' Tao Te Ching
(Translation by Gia-Fu Feng)

THE MIND IS THE MAP, THE BODY IS THE TERRITORY

The organism is a message......We are not stuff that abides, but patterns that perpetuate themselves.

- Norbert Wiener

(The Human Use of Human Beings:

Cybernetics and Society (1950))

From the moment you are born, and even in the womb, everything that you have ever done, seen, heard, smelt, eaten, spoken, thought, touched, felt, given and received is now a part of who you are. These are the essential, undeniable ingredients that create your uniqueness, your originality, your life. Being composed of 75% water the bodies memory is intrinsically connected to the inherited evolving memory of mankind on a cellular level, as well as the accumulated memory of its own lifetime. Your body tells the story of who you are and is the storehouse of all your subconscious and conscious experiences on physical, emotional and psychological levels. It has its own way of memorizing and storing events, creating patterns of posture and habitual behavior that may remain with you until you consciously change those imprints. This is very much the same way as the cells of a computer disc store data,that remains until we re-program the data-base. Our body-mind mechanism can be viewed as a data base that has one major advantage - the human advantage, the grace and ability *to be aware of itself* and to make choices based on experience, knowledge and desire. To be conscious. Your self-awareness, your conscious awareness, is the key ingredient in the equation of growth and transformation.

Your physical body carries the full potential of your life; the seeds of your ability to regenerate and recreate who you want to be, second by second. We say that an elephant never forgets... In the same way the body never forgets and cannot lie. Its natural responses are instinctual and spontaneous, whereas the mind will tend to create diversions and screens to mask, submerge or filter an experience.

Through the years of our lives we accumulate the memory of many types of experience that effect our emotional, psychological and physical well-being. The scope of responses and stored sensations is vast, where some of our experiences may appear quite insignificant others maybe off the spectrum of our ability to cope. We may know feelings of joy, safety, comfort and love as well as knowledge of fear, pain, danger, guilt and so on. Some intense sensations can be so traumatic that they affect the balance of every aspect of our lives, causing us to maintain levels of tension that can promote serious psychological and physical dis-ease. The memory of the events that have caused us to feel that we must protect ourselves, or hide ourselves, which is one definition for tension, may have been pushed far back into the recesses of the subconscious mind, yet the scars can become imprinted in our psycho-physiology, our emotional responses, our dialogue and body language.

Your body is the body of evidence; the reality of *how* you have lived and how you live *now*. You have only one physical body, its true nature cannot be duplicated or divided, only shared. It reveals the path you have trodden and the energy you have cultivated.

People may act out behavior and mannerisms that are not connected up to their real feelings for all kinds of reasons. Some out of fear and conditioning that can inhibit and numb their true feelings; others out of choice or to manipulate situations and other people. But you cannot sincerely fool yourself. Technology can disguise and clone physical appearances but it cannot disguise the true energy, the cellular and emotional make-up of your body and soul that generates your own unique quality of feelings and sensations whose roots are deep beneath the surface. It is *you* who is born and *you* who lives, and *you* who passes away...You cannot live in another person's body or another's reality.

Great actors cultivate the skill and ability to transform their behavior by studying and imitating character traits, accents and body language, getting under the skin of their roles. Some claim that the imprinting of a characters traits can become so powerful it is hard to stay objective, that they may identify with them subjectively, finding it difficult to restore themselves thereafter. But the imprint can teach them many things, deepening reflection, creating empathy, compassion, and a greater sensitivity. The mark of an actors craft and skill is to maintain a strong personal base, to be grounded in themselves to find balance amidst the complexity of emotions they must convincingly portray. Therefore we hear of many actors requiring long spaces of solitude to find themselves whole again.

Your body is your vehicle and is easily identified by its individuality, solidity, it's form and physical boundaries, yet your mind is characterized by its abstract, imaginative and formless nature. Your mind contains the ability to alter views and perceptions so powerfully that it can transform the way you experience the physical world. On the one hand this can be a great advantage, yet on the other, the mind can become so disturbed that it creates many versions of reality, simultaneously, that serve to submerge or avoid the reality of the physical, bodily experience. The mind is like a great magician; a 'trickster extraordinaire.' The ability of the mind to conjure up, on the deepest subconscious levels, abstractions and diversions can profoundly alter your experience of life.

Consequently, your mind has the ability to separate itself from unwelcome or fearful experiences. On the level of self-preservation the minds power of imagination to create alternate realities, when the experiences of the moment are too harsh to bear, may be an empowering and positive action or create an illusionary state of being. The mind is a formless and multifaceted phenomena, yet is as fragile as the vulnerability of your body.

In the most traumatic of situations, where the vulnerability of the body is characterized by the innocence and inexperience of the mind, the minds ability to split itself from its physical reality can have long-term psychologically damaging results. This is evident in the case of multiple personalities where the power of the mind to escape a reality has so convinced the body that it is not in 'real present time' that no memory exists at all of the harmful experiences. Alternate 'personalities' are created who lead separate 'twilight' lives without any knowledge of the original traumas that have caused the body to suffer such a disassociation.

But the body does not lie. The physical and emotional wounds are still evident, yet buried far away from conscious memory. The mind has escaped but somewhere the body carries the evidence of the physical experience.

This situation is very rare and I simply put this perspective here in order to show you the immense significance the mind wealds over the body in order to protect it from its vulnerability. However, in a more diluted less impressionable form this situation happens often. Many of us disassociate ourselves from our pain or discomfort, avoiding the acknowledgment of suffering, whether that be physical, emotional or psychological. Though this tendency may have served a purpose at one time, as we become more aware and responsible for our well-being we see that this pattern of avoidance only serves to push the struggle deeper inside, where the body has to find places to store this unresolved pain. And 'what resists persists'.

Thoughts carry meaning - Meaning carries feelings - Feelings carry relationship - Relationship is life

Life is undoubtedly about our relationships. Whether these relationships are to your environment, your home, your car, your job or yourself the fact is that we have a relationship to it. We do not exist in isolation. Whatever we do is defined by the context, the environment, and what we do within it. Even if you live and work alone you relate to the elements around you whatever they maybe. Even those who chose to live a hermetic or remote life are still bound by the laws of physics which places the physical body in a natural dynamic with its surroundings. How we *chose* to relate is another matter.

The nature of your thoughts carry a certain vibration which in turn stimulates the release of specific neuro-chemicals and hormones that influence the way we actually feel. Happy and contented thoughts will relax the central nervous system which then creates harmonious vibrations of well-being. These vibrations stimulate the body to manufacture essential chemicals through the ductless glands of the endocrine system. As they flow throughout your body via the bloodstream to all your organs and muscles these neuro-chemicals contain the ingredients that alter your bio-chemistry, sending messages of well-being to the body, mind and emotions.

This whole process serves to regenerate your blood cells thereby boosting the immune system and improving your overall health.

Every thought that flows through our minds carries a symbolic meaning. Each word is associated with an experience that conjures up images and feelings that have a certain significance to us individually and collectively. Within our minds we have a library of memories that not only store language but all the associating sensations, imagery and life.

One of the greatest teachings I received on this truth was from a man I met during his fourteenth year in prison. At the tender age of 19 years old this man, (who I shall call Adam here for the sake of his privacy,) found himself undertaking a life sentence for manslaughter. The background details are not important though I found it interesting that he had developed teaching skills in Marshal Arts and other eastern fighting disciplines in his teens before being convicted. Due to the level of maturity already in his heart he had married young and fathered two children. The circumstances in which I met him were in themselves extraordinary. Adam was at that time completing a correspondence yoga teaching training course and required one to one sessions in order to receive the qualification. One of my yoga students at the time had met him as she worked in creating opportunities for further education in prisons and asked me if I'd be willing to teach one to one yoga in a prison. Following an initial meeting with Adam we set up a series of sessions so that I could go into the prison for 2 - 3 hours of practice once a month.

I may have gone as the teacher but it was I who was the student. My experience with Adam showed me how completely subjective our reality is. Not only was his physical level of yogic ability extremely skillful, his inner energy flowed with a dynamic positivity that literally cut through walls. The development of his consciousness had been wrought out of the deep desire to be free of suffering on every level. Adams practice had transformed his prison cell into a clear space for mental, emotional and physical confirmation, purification and liberation.

The power of his commitment, of his desire to use his circumstances to truly transform himself and his reality from a hardship into a blessing had overcome the pressures inherent within that confinement. You may find it difficult to imagine even the thought of one week in a cell yet Adam had softened his heart, strengthened his mind and freed his spirit through fourteen years of imprisonment.

He told me that all the other 'lifers' who came in with him and got to know during his sentence, had either gone completely insane, become addicted to drugs, committed suicide, or when released, had reoffended and been put back inside. I feel a deep respect and admiration for Adams' faith in himself. He showed that the core value in yoga is to love yourself. To completely accept and forgive your body and mind for the pain it may be in and for the suffering it may have caused. Forgiving yourself first, and asking for forgiveness; letting go of the guilt, the blame, the shame and the sorrow yet taking responsibility for the pain you may have caused in order to grow, change and transform. To practice being present with the mind of gratitude for the life you have no matter where you are. His energy carries a special light which he extended out to many others in his situation, wardens and prisoners alike, to help transform the purpose of all their realities, including my own.

ॐ

THE JOURNEY OF YOGA cultivates an on-going awareness of your minds relationship with your body. How you feel about it, treat it, view it, and care for it, is influenced by the passage of yoga in all its many guises. Yoga is a process of reconciliation. A Body Prayer. An expression of balance that intelligently integrates the vulnerability of the body with the caring and meditative focus of your mind. It is therefore, a form of healing, and of prayer that generates qualities of sensitivity, deep relaxation and composure which overflows into your everyday life, touching the very heart of things.

As we become more comfortable within ourselves, we discover an evolving appreciation for life and maturing qualities of self-acceptance. This naturally helps to dissolve any resistance to letting go of tensions that we may be unconsciously holding. Resistance can be a form of apprehension, or fear of feeling the reality of our body as this may access emotional or psychological associations that we would prefer to forget. Yet what resists, persists. What we cannot face or let go of, will often become more imbedded into the internal posturing of ourselves and may be the cause of limitations on our potential for good health and happiness.

Yoga addresses the needs of your body for movement, stillness and alignment with the needs of your mind for psychological satisfaction and balance. The balanced integration of your body and mind naturally nourishes your emotional well-being. And as one thing leads to another, your spiritual nature, your sense of soul and 'belonging' is affirmed in this steady and relaxed inner environment that practice creates. Yoga can give you a direct experience of the ongoing creation of your body as it lives in present time; into a familiar sense of coming home to your undivided self-nature.

Imagine your body is like a musical instrument that when played with technical skill and knowledge produces the kind of harmony, rhythm and vibration that is the perfect music to set you free. Your body has been miraculously equipped with all the strings attached and the practices and disciplines of yoga are designed to harmonize your inner being for optimum benefits. Yoga attunes your body with your mind and subtle energy, taking into consideration all the complexities of your psychological and emotional conditioning.

In order to transform ourselves, we first choose to embrace the myriad of feelings and sensations that are naturally happening within us. We can then integrate into the experience of being who we actually are. For there, lie the seeds of our liberation, hidden amongst the accumulation and drama of life ready to be seen, felt and accepted. Ready to be let go.

THE INTENTION OF
BREATHING

Are you looking for me? I am in the next seat.
My shoulder is against yours.
You will not find me in stupas, not in Indian shrine rooms,
nor in synagogues, nor in cathedrals:
not in masses, not kirtans,
not in legs winding around your own neck,
nor in eating nothing by vegetables.
When you really look for me, you will see me instantly—
you will find me in the tiniest house of time.
Kabir says: Student, tell me what is God?
He is the breath inside the breath.

-Kabir
Translated by Robert Bly

Are you breathing? Yes, of course you are. Can you feel the impulse, the bodies signal to breathe? Your breath is the only involuntary bodily function that you can voluntarily control and directly connects you up with this physical reality. It is the primal link between your birth and the present moment. You breathe in and you breathe out—it happens all by itself yet you are also in control of its passage. Quite simply, being aware of your breath puts you in touch with your life, with the moment, with yourself.

The importance of your breath has many associations and connections that influence the balance of your body, mind and soul and is intrinsic to the practice of yoga. The depths and levels through which it influences the conscious, subconscious and superconscious mind is profound. Due to the primary role your breath takes within the practice of yoga its helpful to know some basic facts about your respiratory system and explore more subtle depths.

THE ANATOMY OF THE BREATH

The breath is your link to the environment in which we live. You know that without the ability to breathe in the oxygen that is freely available (at least at the moment) in our atmosphere, you would not be consciously alive. The breath and life itself can be seen as being one experience. Many things can go wrong with the body and mind, yet we still survive, but when the breath goes life goes as we know it.

As we are rarely taught how to breathe correctly,

unhealthy breathing habits are common. Most people tend to breathe only into the upper lung which puts pressure on the heart and weakens the full functioning of your lungs due to lack of use. The whole body is short changed by shallow breathing which greatly impairs the vitality and energy within the body and mind creating many common psycho-somatic problems such as asthma, high blood pressure, heart disease, low energy, headaches, panic attacks, poor circulation, constipation, insomnia, nervous tension and depression, to name just a few of the endless list of associated imbalances.

Many people inhale and exhale through the mouth, instead of the nostrils. This poor quality of breathing bypasses the physiological inner structure that has naturally evolved to nourish and balance your whole system.

By breathing deeply through your nostrils vital nutrients and oxygen are taken into the full capacity of the lungs via the throat, then the windpipe, and finally to the bronchi in the right and left lung. The lungs then give up the oxygen to the red blood cells which carry it throughout your whole body depositing the oxygen as it goes. During this journey toxic waste in the form of carbon dioxide is picked up by the blood which you then exhale out when the blood returns to the lungs.

Your nose also serves as an air filtering system in the form of tiny nostril hairs which catch some of the dust particles and other pollutants, preventing them from entering your body. Breathing through the nose stimulates a variety of important responses. Your sense of smell, for example, is a primal survival instinct which can trigger emotional states that informs us of likes and dislikes, possible danger and pleasurable experiences. This sense of smell is located in the frontal lobe of the brain which contains the limbic system that also stores our short and long term memory and other survival instincts such as thirst, hunger and sexual drives.

Have you ever noticed how your thinking is reflected in your breathing patterns and acts just like a barometer? Erratic or anxious thoughts will speed up your breathing, whereas relaxed thoughts will slow your breathing down. The reverse is also true. When you deepen and slow your breathing down, your thoughts and feelings will begin to calm and relax. A natural consequence of correct breathing is a heightened sensitivity and a deepening self-awareness.

Breathing charges the electrical currents in and around your body, altering the vibrational energy that feeds your thought processes, heartbeat, physical balance and inner vision. The correct flow of breath into the nasal passages helps to balance the right and left hemispheres of the brain generating more clarity and enriching our inner perceptions.

At the central point, directly between the right and left sides of the brain, resides the pituitary gland, the *third eye* point. This is Ajna, the sixth chakra in alignment with the central Nadi Shushumna, and one of the seven major chakras. The pituitary gland does in fact resemble the shape of an eye, turned on its side, which esoterically has been used as a symbol for intuition, insight and clairvoyance for eons of time. Sometimes it is referred to as the 'all seeing eye' or 'inner eye'. The pituitary gland and pineal gland, which is the seventh chakra Sahasrara, which means 'thousand petaled lotus', are both situated within the brain cavity and are key players in the absorption and regulation of oxygen on a psycho-physiological level, effecting the relationship between the physical, psychological and spiritual qualities of your awareness. They also govern our response to the circadian cycles of night and day and produce important neuro-chemicals that regulate and enrich hormonal balance.

YOUR ABDOMINAL BRAIN

The power of correct breathing directly accesses what is referred to as your 'abdominal brain' or 'hara' (energy center). This is the second chakra known as Svadhisthana located within the region of your Sacral Plexus, the navel. The navel there has an intricate network of nerves which influence the management of our energy resources on a physical as well as subtle level. This center acts like a battery that stores and accumulates energy for future use, recharging your body and mind, and sustaining you during times of strain.

Yet it is also the storehouse or 'waste ground' of undigested waste, tired misdirected energy and associated images that can fester and block the healthy circulation of fresh energy or *Shakti, vital creative energy.*

Your abdominal brains' direct physical links with the navel also carries the memory of your separation from your mother via the umbilicus. This energy center responds with powerful spontaneity to emotional stimuli throughout our lives. During times of stress or conflict this is often the first place to react, and imbalances that affect our digestion and elimination are well known. Most recently medical research has identified 'abdominal migraines' which are common in children whose mental faculties are not as developed as most adults. Studies of these conditions have shown that they are triggered by agitated nerves which generate a *hyper-acidity* in *the bloodstream* and can also be triggered *by* acidic foods. In yogic philosophy these acidic and spicy foods are called *rajasic* which are recognized as substances which stimulate the nervous system. In a sensitive person this will cause an over stimulation giving rise to unhealthy conditions. Your abdominal brain also governs your digestion and absorption of food.

The magic of breathing deeply is all embracing. The more oxygen and *prana* that you absorb creates a chemistry that actually manufactures more alkalinity within your blood. Relaxation, asanas and meditation also alkaline your blood as they calm your whole system. All forms of tension, whether they be caused by injury, poor posture, anger, jealousy, greed, anxiety or agitation promote high levels of acidity which eventually affect this vital nerve center, weakening its power and magnetism. By breathing deeply you can change your chemistry thereby altering harmful states of body and mind.

By paying attention to the physical aspects of the breath you will naturally become aware of the more subtle sensations. This dynamic can open up hidden or buried parts of your self-nature that may have become trapped or submerged in the tension that poor breathing habits create. Your breath is a catalyst that can transform the way you feel. It acts as a bridge between your body and mind over which energy and insights can pass.

Yoga acknowledges the deeper levels of connection that your breath has in relation to your psychological and emotional experiences. It views this primal area of your body, your abdominal brain, as the most important source of energy within you and many practices are focused here.

Practicing yoga with conscious awareness of your breath completely transforms your practice as you engage and acknowledge the deeper connections within you, awakening hidden parts yourself.

THE DESIRE TO BREATHE

Each breath is totally new and independent, it lives only the moment. Every breath you take is a positive decision affirming your intention to live whether this desire is conscious or unconscious you chose it every time you breathe.

Your Life draws insight from deep within the passage of the breath. From that original desire to draw the breath in and re-create new life. From that primal impulse deep within us all to choose life as we inhale our first breath, as we inhale every breath and our natural intelligence to let go of what we do not need as we exhale. Life can be experienced as a series of breaths. Each breath is new, original and independent yet is intrinsically linked to each breath that has gone before. Your past, your present, your future lies within the passage of your breath.

Each breath you take leads a journey through the moment absorbing the experiences of that moment and imprinting it in our cellular structure, in our form *as our bodies*. The breath carrying prana, carrying oxygen and the 'intention' of that moment creates a certain chemistry that influences the way we feel and our mind states. The intention of your awareness is an important ingredient in the unfolding moment. Intention carries purpose which naturally influences the outcome. When you inhale you breathe in the world. All the impressions of that moment are drawn in and digested.

As you breathe out you express a response, an outgoing relationship to that inhalation. The natural intelligence of your body exhaling that which you do not need, and holding on to what you do or *what you believe* you do. Our conditioning can create unnecessary attachments that block the clear passage of the breath. To be conscious of this passage is to initiate an open relationship with what is there, with what is arising within you. This awareness opens the infinite doorway into past, present and future as one unfolding instant. Following the process of our growing awareness with care and diligence matures your insight into life. And so we are created as the accumulation of conscious and unconscious breaths, lives unfolding.

HOW ARE YOU BREATHING?

Does your breathing feel shallow as if
 you do not have enough air?
Or does your breath feel just right?

Are you breathing through your nose or your mouth?
Unless your sinuses are blocked, close your mouth
And breathe through your nose ....that`s what it is for.

Are you gasping for the next breath?
Or do feel satisfied when you breathe?
Does your breathing feel too fast?
Could you slow it down?
Try this......

Place your right hand on your abdomen
Your left hand on your heart
Notice which hand rises more as you inhale
If your left hand rises more than your right
You need to breathe more deeply
Consciously slow your breathing down
Allow your right hand to be pushed up as you breathe in
and to fall back as you breath out

Are you exhaling completely?
The exhalation is equally as important as the inhalation
Let go of all the breath before you breath in again
Notice if you feel any tightness or tension as you breathe
Let your breathing flow into any discomfort
Let the breath circulate
As you exhale let go of any tension - relax

The path of your breath is often at the pivot of meditation practice and is used as a point of focus. My own introduction to breath awareness meditation and the transformative power of conscious breathing came through practice in Zen Buddhist meditation. Yoga and meditation go hand in hand and there are many ways of uniting these elements that suit different people at different times and when you are ready, can be a compassionate force for healing.

MOUNT SHASTA

HEALED, HAPPY AND REBORN I left the red earth of Colorado for the hub of San Francisco where I lived on and off over the following year and a half. The Californian landscape gloriously supported the emerging spiritual culture that was evident in every aspect of life here, and I found myself part of an unformed tribe of other spiritual warriors who were following the calling of their own hearts. My trail flowed down through Big Sur, Santa Cruz, Santa Monica, Orange County, LA and San Diego, all the way to Baha. Many rare guides of the time were available to meet and I sat with Krishnamurti, Ram Dass and Baba Hari Dass who had taken a vow of silence and not spoken for 30 years. Everyone who had a message of transformation and joy seemed to appear here and revolutionary thinkers like Fritjof Capra and Timothy Leary spoke at unusual public events such as the extraordinary Symposium on Humanity which was held simultaneously in LA, Toronto and London in 1979. Yogi Bhajans, 3HO, Happy, Healthy, Holy Organization of kundalini yoga sikhs were everywhere.

At the Shivananda Yoga Center on Dolores Ave in San Francisco I attended classes each day, with many different teachers whose individual approaches and signature voices gave me an invaluable breadth of experience in teaching styles and *Vedanta,* yogic philosophy. In the evenings I would ride on the tram up to Haight-Asbury to receive the engaging teachings on the Tarot and Kabbalah as taught by Amber Waves, a legend in her own time. Amber was an actress and comedienne who transmitted her diverse knowledge through *Savitri,* which comprises the reams of poetic spiritual love verse that the *The Mother* wrote for *Sri Aurobindo,* her consort. The wisdom, creativity and fun of Ambers' classes taught me more about myself and the passion I had for self-inquiry. The rich concoction of studying Kabbalah and yoga drew me more and more to find out about meditation as a vehicle for life.

My body grew increasingly stronger and I regularly visited Orrs Hot Springs, a purifying natural mineral water hot spring deep in the woods north of San Francisco. Here a very small community of like-minded souls was living in a gracious rustic environment. The pools and pungent air infused new elements into my being, deeply relaxing me and eventually shedding my old city skin so that I was truly reformed from the inside out.

The broad brown open road up to Mount Shasta begins to incline steeply. I am going to find The White Brotherhood, a mythical community of mystical beings who, I believe, live inside this holy mountain. My mind turns over the many stories I have read and imagine them walking slowly, circling the mountain top by candlelight in white robes, chanting, as if in a ritualistic trance. I wonder if these stories are true. I so want to find evidence of a magical consciousness that can assure me that all is well on this earth, in my heart. I am driven by the notion of being an acolyte of universal knowledge, of rare wisdom.

Mount Shasta is a sacred mountain and I am here. Will I meet the White Brotherhood and perhaps even see the UFO's the US Air Force describes? This road is longer than I thought, wider too, with dark mammoth evergreen woods on either side. The violet night creeps in and the darkness falls suddenly like a final curtain creating low shadowy shapes and a shuddering chill in the air. I find a soft spot of richly laden pine needles in a clearing to make a small fire, eat a few seeds and huddle down in my sleeping bag. Ill-prepared for this venture I am cold and hungry. This is not like the Isobel Forest. This is a far older forest and I am dwarfed by the sheer scale of the terrain. Lying on the ground gazing up at the omniscient pine trees, a pale moon floats through to reflect me. I feel like a tiny creature exposed and vulnerable. Gradually a distant sound becomes movement close by, a stealthy rustling in the trees. My heart leaps out of my body, and my throat feels instantly parched. There is loud sniffing and panting. It is dogs, Wild dogs. Coyotes!! Can they smell my fear? I do not want to look but I know I must. There are 3 of them, and they seem shy, unsure, the smoke of the dying embers repelling them. I slowly breathe, silently controlling my heart beat, subduing my fear. I pray to be safe. The coyotes move away and I gratefully pray again - for the dawn.

Feeling cold, hungry and fragile I hitch a lucky ride back to town with a bawdy sleepless, hunter who boasted about his near kills in the night. I was so relieved to see him that the rifles in back of the jeep didn't faze me at all. In the local cafe I open my trusty Spiritual Guide to Planet Earth to find somewhere nearby that appeals, where I might stay. I find Shasta Abbey, a Zen Buddhist monastery. Now, that sounded great.

Arriving at the impressive wrought-iron gates I look up towards the snow covered peak of Mount Shasta and pull an old hanging copper bell. The clear happy toll brings out the gate keeper, an elderly woman in worn black robes who welcomes me with curious politeness. "I would like to know more about your life here and perhaps stay for a while if possible', I venture. 'Yes', she says, and brightly, with a somewhat athletic jaunt to her step, takes me into the quiet, yet active enclosure of the monastery grounds.

The teacher of Shasta Abbey was Kennet Roshi, an English Buddhist nun. The resident, ordained monks and nuns wore traditional robes and had shaven heads. Their welcome was warm and practical offering me guidance in *Zazen* in exchange for some help on building a new wing. On that first day a youthful smiling nun took me into their well-stocked library to show me books and teachings of the Buddha which I had never read before. I felt as though I was reading my own mind. This is how I think! This is me! Yoga had satisfied the needs of my spiritual body..... these teachings inspired my spiritual intellect and nourished my soul. I knew I had found another Teacher.

Leading me into the *dojo* (meditation hall) I felt an immediate sense of belonging. I was shown how to sit, Zazen style, on a zafu and zabuton and given the meditation practice of following my breath. I was left alone in this enormous incense filled space to practice. I loved it. This had to be it. This was the reason I came to Mount Shasta. The White Brotherhood really does work in mysterious ways. This elusive group of spiritual masters, known as The White Brotherhood are spoken about in the teachings of Godfre Ray King in his 1934 book 'Unveiled Mysteries' as being The Ascended Masters who have ascended to a higher dimension from which they guard and help the evolving human race. Saint Germaine was sighted by many spiritual teachers as well as King who claimed to have met him on the slopes of Mount Shasta, and many other sightings on these slopes were documented during the 1930's yet knowledge of the Ascended Masters first arose between 1880 and 1900.

This, my first introduction to Buddhist meditation practice, was a revelation. I felt completely at home with this simple way that held so much mindfulness, richness and fulfillment. This was something real, that I could sense had an authenticity because I became completely absorbed within it. After a few weeks of teachings and practice I had to leave as the ordained practitioners began their annual three month retreat. On returning to San Francisco a friend asked if I would like to go to Hawaii, and within two weeks we were there.

SELF-REMEMBRANCE

AT THIS MOMENT in time you are the sum of the equation of all your past experiences - of your dreams, and of your family inheritance. You are the totality of all that you have lived through since the day that you were born and that which you have inherited from your parents genetically, psychologically and emotionally. Buddhists call it Karma, the law of cause and effect where everything we connect with comes back to us in one form or another. As above, so below.

Closing your eyes you cannot see your body yet you know it is there. Your senses are aware of all your living parts yet you do not think foot, head, arms, and head to know that you are here, unless these parts are in some way uncomfortable. You just are and you know it! In fact you probably very rarely think about it. When you are conscious and awake you exist! When your body is asleep your mind drops away from the physical experience of being alive and temporarily forgets the body unless your senses are disturbed by noise, or temperature or discomfort. Your body is always there for you to identify with and so it is easy to take for granted. Yet this body is a great gift - it gives your life meaning and focus. For it is through your senses, 'through the doors of perception' that you experience the world; that you take the world in and share within it. We come to trust that our bodies will fulfill our needs, desires and intentions. Spontaneously responding we grow to know our weaknesses, our strengths and our handicaps, relying on the body to perform naturally.

Self-remembrance brings us into the moment, uniting our bodies and minds thereby reducing stress and anxiety, which is so often caused by the pressure of having to do one thing whilst thinking about another. Though we are undoubtedly used to performing on various levels at once, the source of our ability needs to be replenished so that we do not run out of steam, which so often happens. This continuous demand to achieve external goals, meet expectations, and juggle many tasks at once leaves little time to enjoy the fundamental consciousness that is holding us together, at the very source of who you are. Extreme conditions such as M.E, also known as Chronic Fatigue Syndrome,that affects every aspect of the body, mind and spirit, is indicative of the kind of burn-out that can happen when we neglect to nourish the inner resources of our energy output on this primary level. Imbalances that affect our psycho/spiritual well-being, as well as the nervous system and immune system manifest in a myriad of ways depending on the personality, genetic inheritance and karmic influences of each individual.

The variety of symptoms whose origins stem from being out of touch with our innate sensibilities is growing at an alarming rate. Illnesses relating to sleeplessness, depression, heart problems, digestive disorders and neurosis of all kinds, are some of the conditions which have a direct connection with this separation we feel from our inner selves. There is only so much disassociation one person can handle before their bio-chemical and instinctual, self-preserving nature will close down and quit!

In the present evolution of our global spiritual consciousness, more of us are finding sanctuary outside of the confines of formal religious doctrine and pre-conceived belief systems. We are searching for new ways to nourish our souls and bring meaning and purpose into our lives. People feeling lost, isolated and alone often fall prey to false 'gods', to so called churches and temples where they suddenly become part of a community that they can 'belong to' but end up being dangerously controlled. With so much misconception and spiritual manipulation leading people astray, it is vital that we learn how to access our own inner truth and sense of connection to the world in which we live, without the cajoling, power struggles of media moguls, political leaders and spiritually colored propaganda.

The following meditation, Self-Remembrance, is food for the soul nourishing your presence of body and mind thereby replenishing the inner core of your life supporting consciousness. This practice can be done at anytime, anywhere, alone or with others. When you remember yourself and become still you step back from the draw of outgoing energy, restore your inner center, building greater self-awareness and purpose. You will naturally tune into the greater scheme of things, the bigger picture where you can appreciate the joy of simply being.

MEDITATION PRACTICE

Reflect for a moment on how you feel right now.
Relax your shoulders and allow your breathing to slow down
Letting each breath satisfy you.
Become very, very still, do not move your body unnecessarily.

Feel the touch of your body on the surface,
Hear the sounds coming in around you,
Notice your eyesight focusing on these words,
Sense any scent that comes to you,
Experience your breath flowing in and out.

Tune in to any other feelings or sensations that are apparent,
Any spontaneous movements or twitch, any discomfort
Parts of yourself where your attention is drawn, whether
physical, emotional or psychological.
Be still. Be present. Remember yourself.
Notice your familiarity with your own presence.
Simply be here in the moment.
Be aware of the totality of yourself

Naturally without straining or effort notice the energy of life
within you,
The feeling of simply being alive and breathing
Being aware of your senses, your presence of mind.
Be here for and as yourself, the space around you
Your senses open and receptive
Remembering yourself saying inwardly
'I am I am I am'

PRANA

The Tao is an empty vessel; it is used, but never filled.
Oh, unfathomable source of ten thousand things!
Blunt the sharpness,
Untangle the knot,
Soften the glare,
Merge with dust.
Oh, hidden deep but ever present!
I do not know from whence it comes.
It is the forefather of the emperors.

-Lao Tsu
'The Tao Te Ching' (6th century B.C.)
Translation by Gia-Fu Feng and Jane English

PRANA EXISTS IN ALL LIVING THINGS but is not
dependent on them, and all living things exist within
prana. It is the pure vital energy that sustains life as we
know it from within and without. This prana is not
your consciousness or spirit, it is simply a form of
energy that flows through all material objects and
subtle forms of manifestation. This includes your

thoughts and feelings, the food you eat and waste you produce. Perhaps we can say that prana is lifes' pure creativity, chi, love in action, or simply grace.

Every cell in your body is imbued with prana. It is in all forms of matter and yet is not matter. Prana is the energy or force that animates all things and gives life. The most powerful source of prana is in the air, yet it is not the oxygen nor any of its other elements. Prana flows through sunlight and water yet it is not heat, or vitamins or light-rays. We absorb prana through the air we breathe, our food and water. Prana is also recognized as universal energy that enters in where air cannot penetrate and manifests as electricity, gravity, nerve currents and thought forms. Yogic science perceives prana as the cause and source of life itself in all its forms. In the human body the most refined level of prana is thought, and the densest level is in the activity of the lungs. The densest form of prana is drawn in through the breath to the lungs enriching our oxygen levels and absorption into the blood stream and through the digestion of fresh food. The most subtle form of prana is in the quality of our consciousness and thought processes that influences our state of mind and well-being.

PRANIC HEALING

All forms of yoga can be defined as pranic healing as the conscious circulation of prana through the Nadis, channels of pranic energy, and through your chakras is the very purpose of practice.

The four forms of yoga, the three branches and eight limbs of yoga discussed later increase the flow of prana, cultivating those different areas of life. People who are consciously developing themselves, detoxifyng, creating peace, meditating and clearing their bodies and minds from harmful vibrations emanate a great deal of prana which naturally benefits all those living around them. Yoga can equalize the flow of energy when consciously practiced.

As prana is so subtle it benefits greatly from direction through your conscious awareness. This means that your mind is the prime mover of pranic energy. When you are in a yoga asana (posture) and feel some tension or resistance you can direct the flow of prana there, by consciously focusing your mind in that area and breathing into it. Prana regenerates and clears blocked energy nourishing your physical body with fresh vitality and healing vibrations. In the same way if you bang your knee you immediately put you hand there and hold your breath. This channels the flow of healing pranic energy to that area.

Yoga seeks to attain balance through the conscious control of prana on every level of your being. The breath, being the most powerful force for channeling prana into the physical body, is structured into techniques known as *pranayama*.

Prana travels into the body via *nadis* which are invisible pathways that connect up with your nervous system and endocrine system influencing your whole being. There are about 72,000 nadis in all and they form an intricate communications network that centers around three main Nadis that govern the spinal energy and central and autonomous nervous system.

Nadis channel prana, like nerve currents, from the physical to the subtle body, and from the subtle to the physical body. Research has shown the power of this connection in situations where a limb or organ has been removed or amputated yet that person continues to experience ongoing sensations of those 'missing' limbs or body parts. The 'psychic' nerve currents that have energized those parts with prana is still flowing, creating a sense, a feeling that those parts are still there. The system of the Nadis is still intact though your physical body may not be. The practice of pranayama naturally works to balance the connections between the physical and subtle body 'renegotiating' the new information for the best possible result, which may be to redirect the flow of prana elsewhere or to maintain the 'psychic' impression within your senses. Your bodies' natural intelligence and desire to feel good will be activated through pranayama to make the best decision.

Ida is the feminine nadi, and creates a cooling flow of energy within you, symbolized by the moon. Pingali is the male nadi, creating a hot flow of energy symbolized by the sun. Together these two channels act as one, maintaining a temperate environment that also balances the right and left hemispheres of the brain, characterized in a similar way. The left brain can be described as male outgoing energy defined by the word *Assertive*. The right side of the brain is the feminine hemisphere, can be described as *Reflective*.

Ida and Pingali Nadis originate in the base of the spine, rising up each side of the vertebrae, culminating at the center of the forehead, the sixth chakra Ajna, the third eye point. And then rises up into the seventh crown chakra Sahasrara, which is a source of light and consciousness.

The central Shushumna nadi is activated by intense and consistent practice of pranayama and other pranic techniques. Yet also Shushumna can be awoken through 'Bhakti' devotional Love and the maturing of conscious grace which is a blessing that imbues your body, mind and soul with the energy and awareness to receive this dynamic flow of what can be described as a spiritual awakening. The power of this awakening can be so intense that unless your body and mind have been strengthened and opened up over time on very deep levels of awareness, it can be a shock for the body and mind as it breaks through so much conditioning which may be held unconsciously. This is why working with a teacher who can guide you carefully through such a deep practice is so important. Shushumna nadi is stimulated by the awakening Kundalini energy that usually lies dormant in the base of the spine and is symbolically depicted as a serpent. If it is aroused its dynamic power can travel up the spine to Sahasrara, the seventh crown chakra, opening the third eye in its wake. Some say it can 'blow your mind' or if you are well attuned can awaken you completely immersing you in pure consciousness. This is why the autonomic nervous system, as well as the spinal vertebrae and connective tissue, needs to be strong and healthy in order to sustain the force of the awakened kundalini.

PRANIC DOORWAYS

In a sense your whole body is a pranic doorway. You could say that you are the world as when you are not here, not conscious of your senses, you cannot be sure or even know that this world exists. You are a totality within yourself with physical boundaries, a unique past and an ongoing personal evolution. It is your interaction with the world via your energy going out and receiving energy coming in that you generate your life. This coming and going of energy is motivated by prana. In fact your whole body is one great mass of prana vibrating at various levels of intensity and creativity according to the way you think, feel, move and act.

Within your body there are strategic power centers or openings where pranic energy has direct influence on us and through which we can cultivate and control its benefits. Nadis are concentrated in these areas, increasing the information channeling through. Like any system there needs to be stations, banks or resource centers whereby you can gain access and control of the workings and operations of that system. And like all stations they can be very busy, congested or malfunctioning to the point of a standstill, due to lack of organization and awareness of what is needed to help that station operate at an optimum level of efficiency. When one station is out of balance, it usually impacts on the whole flow of energy throughout the network. So we seek to find balance through all the pranic doorways and experience a smooth ride.

These key doorways are known as *Chakras* (wheels) which are vortexes of dynamic energy that link up your subtle energy with your physical experiences. Subtle energy includes your thought processes, intentions, feelings, dreams, spiritual awareness, your electro-magnetic field, vibration and psychic impressions.

Interpretations of the chakras have been well documented that show the relationship these pranic doorways have with your body, mind and emotions. The key words used to symbolize the qualities within each chakras describe the essence and purpose of that sphere.

You will notice that these seven energy centers correspond with the seven endocrine glands that secrete their hormones and neuro-chemicals directly into the blood stream. The relationship between these two systems is discussed in the piece on *'psycho-neuro-immunology'* in this book. *Pranayama* and meditation on the chakras further enriches your understanding and practice of how yoga can benefit your whole life. Focusing on these energy centers accelerates the influx of prana as a force for healing.

Breathing serves many purposes besides being the fundamental thread linking birth to death and functions as a bridge between your body and mind over which fresh energy travels freely. Breathing re-charges the electrical currents in and around the body, balancing the vibrational messaging that regulates the heart-beat, calming the nervous system, improving physical balance and your sensitivity of sensory awareness. The correct flow of prana via the nasal passages and 'Nadis,' helps to re-balance right and left hemispheres of the brain generating more clarity thereby enriching your cognitive and intuitive perception.

The flow of breath has many associations and connections that influence the relationship between the body, mind and emotions yet despite being fundamental to our existence is largely untapped as a source for healing. The depth through which breathing influences the conscious and subconscious mind is a science within itself and is at the very core of Ayurveda and Yoga, practiced as Pranayama, breathing techniques, and Pranic Healing. The form and techniques of pranic healing can be interpreted in different ways yet the process is always to open the channels of conscious connection to the flow of life energy within and around you.

The benefits of conscious breathing are all embracing. The increased intake of prana becomes an organic medicine that can transform your physical well-being as well as the nature of your psycho-spiritual experience. When high levels of oxygen and prana are absorbed this generates an internal chemistry that produces more neutralizing, calming Alkalinity to circulate through your bloodstream enriching the quality of your blood cells, reducing inflammation and regenerating visceral tissue. This is your natural internal pharmacy of bio-chemical change and regeneration boosting healing and reducing symptoms of stress. This naturally helps you to feel more uplifted, elevated and happier which enriches your sense of gratitude and appreciation for life, a sign of good health.

The cycle of repair is also stimulated by generating happy, creative and peaceful thoughts that equally relax the central nervous system creating harmonious vibrations of well-being. These vibrations then trigger the body to manufacture essential hormones through the ductless glands of the endocrine system. As these hormones flow throughout your body via the bloodstream to all the organs and muscles they become neuro-chemicals that contain the ingredients that alter your chemistry restoring healthy genes. This whole process in turn purifies your lymphatic system via the blood cells thereby boosting the immune system, strengthening your ability to naturally detox and overcome many kinds of common infection or ill health. Your overall immunity becomes more effective through changing life conditions and environments.

On the other hand, all forms of tension or negativity, whether caused by injury, pain, poor posture, anger, jealousy, sadness, depression, anxiety or stress can produce toxic levels of agitation in the form of neuro chemicals such as cortisol or adrenaline that creates Acidity in the bloodstream, which eventually deteriorates the physical bodily tissue damaging the efficiency of many bodily functions. Acidity is degenerative and corrosive, causing inflammation, weakening connective tissue, digestion, elimination, bones viscera and most importantly the innate power of healing potential and regeneration within you. These acidic conditions can also affect the balance of the brain as the nutrients required to think with clarity are depleted and may manifest as loss of patience, sleeplessness, poor concentration and depression amongst many other psychological imbalances.

PSYCHO-NEURO-IMMUNOLOGY

This very interesting term '*psycho-neuro-immunology*' was formed by Western neuro-scientists who have made significant breakthroughs in identifying that there are actual bio-chemical links between our psychology (the way we think), the nervous system and the endocrine glands which secrete their hormones and neuro-chemicals directly into the blood stream, some of which govern our immune system and therefore the healthy functioning of our immunity. Our immune systems' main function is to protect and cleanse, boosting the bodies' ability to fight off infections and viruses to which the human organism is organically susceptible. Though the connection of our psychological and emotional wellbeing to the immune system is relatively new to Western thinking, this knowledge has been the foundation of Yogic philosophy for centuries. Yoga is based on the understanding that all the internal activities of the body and mind are intrinsically connected and therefore the importance of acknowledging the wellness of the whole person is essential in order to achieve optimum health and wellbeing.

Yoga has always been viewed as a science as well as a life path, a philosophy, and so it is of great benefit to this work that western research is validating the ancient wisdom inherent within the practice of yoga. This is where science meets spirituality in a very visceral way.

Significant change happens when the body and mind are in repose, in a relaxed and receptive state of being. Consider that stillness is not the absence of movement, it is in fact a fertile and nourishing environment for psychological and emotional integration. Movement is the *forerunner* of change. Real change occurs in the midst of seeming stillness when energy is vibrating at such an intensely subtle level, that it can only be perceived through the internal environment of the senses and not the physical eye. Here you have the space and pause to perceive, reflect and accept the sensations of change that are arising. The relationship of the body-mind integrates change through stillness allowing the body to transform itself naturally with significance.

In deep states of relaxation and meditation Theta Waves have been monitored flowing from the brain, which signify a calm, highly attuned, aware yet detached quality of consciousness that can also be interpreted as a transcendent state of mind. These Theta Waves influence the internal pharmacy of your miraculous human form to manufacture and distribute dynamic neuro chemicals and hormones such as Serotonin and Endorphins that give positive, uplifting and elevated feelings to our whole being forming harmonious waves of restoration.

A sense of fulfillment and contentment can arise and it is within this composed internal environment that the molecules of your psychological, emotional and physical make up have an opportunity to naturally re-align, restructure and rebuild themselves. This is the purpose of Savasanna, the Asana of Repose known as Corpse Pose when prana is fully integrated and saturates your being and beyond post any yoga practice.

Realize that your breath is a key to unlock the passage to peace. It is always there for you as a friend and ally. The breath is the inner mistress of the master yogi and yogini. You have given birth to the breath and the breath has given birth to you; your consciousness.

AN INTERIOR LANDSCAPE

Facing myself facing

a white-washed wall

Breathing my parent's sadness

Still silence falling into a bottomless well

Of bare emotion

where sorrow lines the walls

And the cave am I that echoes the memory

Of those narrow moments

When the slightest gesture would have consoled.

-Myself

How long have I been sitting here, breathing. My face wet and stinging with the salts of ancient tears- ancient hours - that flow straight from the sea of remembrance. The sea of love. I am so comfortable here. I remember this feeling well, from somewhere else; when was it? Maybe it was a dream. Have I always been here, in this place where others tread so carefully, preserving peace; bells sounding the structure of time? Hands join in gassho, palms meeting at my heart, eyes half cast, I stand up alongside others all breathing, all moving as one, bowing to the white-washed wall so innocently reflecting my mind.

Breathing, stepping, I have come to love the sound of rain, hard on the worn tin roof, softly entering the sphere of my hearing mind. Tap, tap, tap, tap… I kneel at the head of a robed row of kindred spirits, awaiting the sound of the gong to lead me to meet a gentle man of expanded calm, of deep composure, of sensibility. A smile so wry, so full of comprehension, leaking wit, I sit before him in the breeze of his presence. Aitkin Roshi. Candle light, incense, and breath… Darshan. 'Who is breathing? You are a hair's-breath away.' Gassho. We bow to one another.

The white-washed wall receives me. Breathes me. Ahh, the comfort of this place, the familiarity of my soul, my sanity. This zafu! This pure simplicity defines me.

Forgive me, my mind, I only forgot temporarily, I never was lost, I am here for you - for me!

Nothing to lose, nothing to gain. I just found a place I already knew. How lucky am I, far from home I find my true home, in the sound of rain on a tropical tin roof.

MAUI ZENDO sits in the lush tropical district of Haiku in Maui Hawaii, a fitting name for such a sublimely poetic place. I was literally swept up to the Zendo by divine intervention as a powerful hurricane hit the island the day I arrived and lasted for three days. We found refuge in the hills away from the shore and this is exactly where the wind had blown me. It had once been a discreet and exotic geisha house for rich Japanese business men. The wood floors shone with a natural elegance and circular glass windows framed the tropical scenery outside. Situated in a lofty spot high in the Maui Hills you could see all the way out to the ocean and beyond to limitless sky. The seasons were punctuated by rainfall and morning chill, but the endless summer warmth maintained a divinely pleasant atmosphere for all living things.

My first seven-day *sesheen* meditation retreat was just beginning as I arrived to this sacred place. The poem above came from this experience and heralded in a grateful appreciation of meditation that is still with me as I write and grow into the autumn of my life.

I am sitting on a little stool next to my mother and sister in our long, beautifully furnished blue and gold sitting room. All the mirrors have been completely covered with large drapes and people are milling around, crying, and reaching out to me. I am wearing a long, chestnut-brown corduroy Laura Ashley dress that I love, that protects me like a monk's habit. I feel like a dark, lost cloud. Heavy with rain, heavy with guilt, condensed by the pressure of so many faces searching mine for answers; answers to questions that I do not understand. I speak a different language, one that is submerged beneath the irony of being a teenager fighting for emotional independence and the co-dependent loss of my parent. I do not know what to say, or what to feel. How to respond to the tsunami of grief that floods every atom of oxygen around and within me. I appear here in body, yet my mind and spirit have absconded for refuge in a place I do not know, that is hidden from my responsibility to respond; from my sense of belonging. Men are praying in the ancient language of my forefathers, rocking piously back and forth and my mother weeps with other women, some soft, some strong.

The polished baby grand piano sits solemnly at the far end of the room as if waiting to be heard, and my gaze goes to my fathers' well-stocked bar at the other end where Patsy, his dearest friend props up one side. She was born into a different faith where grieving is not expressed so ritually and with far less drama. I have always been close to her and I move over to her side where we drink sweet red kiddush prayer wine together in a heavily burdened silence. We reach for one another every now and then, embrace and pour another drink.

There is movement outside the room and I am ushered into our dining room where my mother is shrieking and tearing her sweater. The old and wizened sun-scorched rabbi's wife tells me that it is tradition for the wife to tear her clothing over her husband's open coffin to express her grief. I am stunned by the exposure of my fathers composed face, and the heat of the room, the tears and wrenching cries. I cannot breathe but stay there as I am too heavy to move, too sad for my mother, whose grief reaches a part of me I do not know, cannot recognize, and I am freezing over like Alaska. I am hiding somewhere far away from the pain of remembrance.

At sixteen my father died at a time when we were not on good terms. Our relationship had degenerated through what seemed then to be our vast differences of opinion. Being a strong willed and explorative person I had left home very early to travel the world and find my own education. In fact, I had run away at one time and caused harrowing anxiety for my parents which also brought me into experiences so prematurely that I could not share them with anyone. The accumulation of so much grief and loss for my father formed an unapproachable distance and lingering sadness between us.

We loved each other but could not accept each other's differences. When he passed on we were still struggling on the battlefield of our emotional wills and I did not have the opportunity to make friends with him or tell him I loved him before he died. Raw anger arose in me at his death which I aimed at the doctors who I felt had mistreated him and vowed to learn to heal in my life-time. This anger was, of course, my own pain for not having reached him myself or made the difference between life and death, between peace and war, between father and daughter. Yet it was this vow that began the journey I was destined to travel. The healing I wanted to give was the healing of my own life and the sharing of love that comes from this. Years later I was to go through this healing with my father within the sanctity of a silent, three month meditation retreat.

Young and wild at heart I was not aware of the tremendous impact my father's death had on my emotional body and in my heart. A dam opened up within me pouring out the vast sea of love and sadness of the past. When I began to meditate at Maui Zendo dreams with the clarity of cut-glass filled my silent nights. Many were embellished with vivid visions of gazing into clear turquoise pools through which I could see my own reflection and the sandy waterbed beneath. All the sadness that had been buried or frozen within my emotional body flowed out to be recognized in this new home of awareness that meditation had given to me. Like the prodigal son, I had truly arrived home, to a place that was new yet familiar, a place I had forgotten. The irony was that I had traveled to the other side of the planet to glean this insight and yet my breath had been there for me all the time. My awareness had opened to touch the hurt and sadness hidden deep inside. I was being initiated into the lost land of my family inheritance, the connection to my parents, my birth, even before my birth to a sense of my original unchanging nature.

The Diamond Sangha on Maui, Hawaii was lead by Aitkin Roshi, a grand teacher of the Soto Zen tradition who had been ordained with Yamado Roshi in Japan where he lived as part of that Sangha. Aitkin Roshi embodied an elegant stance and lucid mind. His non-interfering wisdom during these formative years of my practice was an example within itself. Sometime later in Japan, I sat with other monks and teachers whose vibratory qualities and ceremonious style embroidered my cloth of understanding with the origins of this cultural discipline. For many years I breathed and sat in meditative silence at the Maui Zendo, a Zen Buddhist lay community of fellow practitioners. My life there revolved around daily practice, *sesheen* (retreats), silk painting, batiking and community work.

Maui Zendo was the first real school I had ever been to, where deep respect, mindfulness and compassion were being cultivated. There was purpose here and the solitariness suited my growth. I loved Zazen. The refinement of the environment, the practice dojo, the poetic teachings, the discipline and the form all appealed to my aesthetic senses as well as the calling of my heart and mind for tranquility. This was a place where I could truly listen.... hear the sound of my own thoughts, my breath, the Hawaiian wind and rain. As the years went by I absorbed and wholly appreciated this orchestrated life and intensity of practice. There, Jutta Hahne, a unique and statuesque fellow practitioner who took care of Roshi taught me how to batik, simply by watching her artistic excellence on many happy afternoons. My skills in batiking and silk painting developed fast and I created exotic hand sewn kimonos that were sold and exhibited locally on the island and people would visit me from all over to order special commissions for themselves or as gifts. I recall an abundance of fulfilled, warm, breezy days in my wooden hut in the Eucalyptus Grove. The smell of hot bees-wax, ready for batiking that I had bought from the bee-keeper down the road, embedded with poor dead bees that were drained away after the wax had melted. I batiked images of the beauty all around me; bamboo, banana leaves, hibiscus flowers, birds of paradise, long wild grasses, sunsets and moon scenes. Dying the silks in bright radiant colors and hanging them out to dry, watching the breeze flow through them. Then sitting quietly for hours stitching the pieces together whilst listening to the sound of the wind, birds and leaves. This utopia was a very special time of my life and I cannot find words to express the gratitude for the blessings I received during those five magical years. I began to read and write more poetry and one of my favorites has always been Ryokan, the 17th century Japanese Zen monk.

ZAZEN MEDITATION PRACTICE

Too lazy to be ambitious,
I let the world take care of itself.
Ten days' worth of rice in my bag;
a bundle of twigs by the fireplace.
Why chatter about delusion and enlightenment?
Listening to the night rain on my roof,
I sit comfortably, with both legs stretched out.

- Ryokan

ZAZEN MEDITATION PRACTICE is a simple process of breath awareness. The principle of the technique stems back many hundreds of years and brings the focus of the mind in direct contact with the subtle and present experience of breathing. The breath counting of Zazen reveals the importance of anchoring the mental concentration to the subtle nature of the breath so that the mind will have something present, spontaneous, yet tangible to focus on. The nature of the mind likes to be engaged and occupied and if not given a repetitious practice to do, will wander away from the present moment making it much harder to harness. All meditations serve to bring us into the moment by moment reality of ourselves, growing into ever deeper levels of awareness as our concentration develops in continuity. This is a wonderfully relaxing and regenerative meditation which helps us to integrate body and mind thereby creating a calm center of attention.

The benefits of practice generally clear the mind of excess activity, improve overall concentration and focus, stabilize and ground our hearts emotionally, where we become less reactionary yet more responsive. This brings a sense of inner repose to our communication, a lighter spirit and happier disposition.

Zazen is based on the compassionate philosophy of *Beginners Mind*. Beginners Mind represents the reality of *each, new* moment, holding exactly the same potential for insight and realization as the moment before or the moment to come. That the breath only lives *in the moment*, in the here and now, and so consequently follows that every moment contains the same opportunities. This compassionate understanding also frees us from unnecessary attachments to the past and any pain or suffering that this may ensue.

Beginners Mind also helps us to bring a fresh spirit

to our meditation practice each time we realize that the mind has wandered off or is day dreaming and is no longer focused on the breath. As soon as we realize this we simply start to count at 'one' again with the renewed quality of attention. We always have another chance. This is Zen Mind, Beginner Mind.

Though not part of this meditation it is interesting to know that the practice of zazen also embraces Koan Study. Koans are seemingly cryptic, esoteric and remarkably profound questions such as 'Who is Breathing?' or 'What was your face before you were born?', which are given by the teacher to each individual student and contemplated during zazen, and in fact, at any time. However, the purpose of all zazen meditations are the same in that they point to the awakening of your 'original self-nature', or Buddha Nature, that is unchanging and beyond name, time and space.

Zen is full of parallels, contradictions and poetic analogy. The Koan *Do not mistake the pointing finger for the moon*, is a beautiful reflection of the tendency of the mind to identify with the *form* of practice, and miss the point!

It is best to practice zazen sitting with a straight spine, whether you are in a chair or on a cushion or zafu, cross-legged, kneeling or in half lotus. But any posture will do if you are unable to sit upright. Practice for 25 minutes morning and evening.

ZAZEN MEDITATION

Bring your hands to rest one upon the other at your abdomen or in your lap, your right hand resting in the palm of your left hand, the thumb tips touching. Relax your shoulders, elbows and wrists.

Your eyes are half cast, slightly looking down.
Let your inner face gently smile.
Find that point within you that desires to breathe
The point at which your body draws the breath in
And let it go.
Do not force the breath in any way.
Just notice when you spontaneously breathe
And let it happen all by itself.
You may find the breath in your belly
Or around your solar plexus.
Wherever you feel it, focus your mind there.
When you have established awareness of your breath
Begin to count rounds of ten breaths.
One count is a whole inhale and exhalation.
Wait for the breath to happen naturally
Then count it.
Inhaling, exhaling ✍ one
Inhaling, exhaling ✍ two

And so on

You do not need to force the breath, you will instinctively breathe.

When you get to ten, go back to one again.
If you find that you have lost count & are thinking about other things
Don't worry, this happens
Just go back to one and begin again.
This is Zen mind, beginners mind
where we always begin again.
Every breath a new breath.

Sitting quietly, doing nothing, the grass grows by itself.

THE BODY OF
CONSCIOUSNESS

When grapes turn
to wine, they long for our ability to change.
When stars wheel around the North Pole,
they are longing for our growing consciousness.
Wine got drunk with us,
not the other way.
The body developed out of us, not we from it.
We are bees,
and our body is a honeycomb.
We made the body, cell by cell we made it.

-Jalaluddin Rumi (1207-1273)
Translated by Robert Bly

OUR SEARCH FOR BELONGING, for being part of a
greater whole, becomes the predominant theme as we
grow into our teens and most people will experiment

with ways of losing themselves to find a new identity. We want to break through our inhibitions, our social moorings and tensions and many people turn to alcohol, drugs and the power of music as agents of transformation. We seek to over-ride the boundaries of our physical bodies and the conditioning in our minds to access a personal freedom, a real sense of happiness. We want instant change and this fundamental draw to transcend what appears to be reality speaks volumes about our instinctual aspirations and intentions. We seek to empty ourselves of the pressure to be 'someone' and just have fun and enjoy life. We may even attempt to completely obliterate or annihilate ourselves, so that we no longer feel separate, do not feel bound by the physical laws of nature and are united with … well, we are not sure what, but it feels like the sea of humanity. Addiction to the miss use of such intoxicants is a tragic part of our universal culture. Even food may become a drug which can cause feelings of 'obliteration' and obsessions relating to abusing the existence of the body such as obesity or anorexia are a growing social disease.

We all want to lose ourselves in one way or another and many of us have experimented with ways of reducing *or* expanding the distance between us and the world, depending on how you see it! We feel the urgency to take quantum leaps into the unknown so that we can disassociate ourselves from too much familiarity, from the boredom of loss of inspiration. Losing control and returning to a vulnerable spontaneity can release enormous stress and many forms of holistic therapies are based on this premise that facilitate people letting go of habitual control patterns. Cultural history and religious tribal ceremonies often employ the transformative power of psychedelic plants and ritualistic dance as a way to transcend the seeming human limitations of form and personality opening to a more intuitive and spiritual wisdom of understanding. Shamanism and some tantric traditions are rich with references to the use of intoxicants as a way of overcoming feelings of separation and magnifying the senses.

The union of sexuality is undoubtedly a primary experience for satisfying this longing, this desire to lose ourselves in an all embracing way. At the peak of sexual experience we feel a profound vulnerability and timelessness that elevates us into a natural freedom, an ego-less-ness, that is powerfully liberating. On one level it is purely sensory and on another sexual union can open the gates of a deeper connection to ourselves and to our partners. We lose our separate identity and identify with the other. We experience a unity, yet a freedom, within a natural sense of belonging. There is suddenly no 'other', no definition or place where you end and your partner begins. When two become one.

As a life-affirming expression of our human condition, sexuality is genetically imprinted in our psycho-physiology to merge and make that primal connection with another human being. An orgasm is the antithesis of the competitive and materialistic lifestyle that typifies modern society and is a primal, unchanging experience that draws from the very essence of our humanity. True sexual intimacy can take us beyond the periphery of ourselves into realms of unimaginable joy, deep relaxation, passion and even transcendence. For many people sexual experience may be the only way they are able to effectively release themselves from physical, emotional and psychological tension. Yet, of course, this expression is much more than just releasing tensions through our highly charged nervous system or to create children.

Tantra yoga is the cultivation and refinement of sexual unity providing a pure and natural form for deepening our evolving self-awareness through dissolving the sense of separation from others by false conditioning and other egoic inhibitions. We are put in touch with our own and our partner's powerful, primal sensuality within a cauldron of elemental fire and water. With the right partner, where the chemistry of love and attraction is truly present, these practices can quickly take us beyond identification with the body, intensifying feelings of freedom and liberation that transcends even the interpretation of the intellect.

Deepening our sensitivity and spiritual empathy awakens our higher consciousness transforming sexual union into an ecstatic and healing experience. Total intimacy requires courage, trust and surrender that all challenge the construct of the mind, yet are familiar territory for the heart. The heart, body and mind are fully engaged at once. Here again, the body becomes the key, the channel through which we break through the fears and boundaries that have built walls to lock in and keep out the risk of exposure, and free ourselves into our spontaneous, boundless joy.

THE ONLY WAY OUT IS THROUGH

IN THE THROES OF my search for peace, for reconciliation and for belonging I was lucky enough to come across yoga practices that gave me the feelings I was looking for. I have learnt that your body is a temple, a sacred space of freedom and belonging, and that its miraculous form is transformable and mutable when you embrace its totality. Meaning that your body, your form, and all that goes on within it, is a holy place which you can enter and discover the mystery of how to rise above its seeming confines. You cannot avoid this truth once you have entered the palace of consciousness.

What you discover may surprise you as this process

of entering the portal of your senses, simply reveals that your essential nature is an intimately familiar quality that has been there all along. For it is you. It is you at home, in the sanctuary of your own love and surrender. In the safety of your inner most self and sanity, feeling perfectly acclimatized to the ongoing changes that characterize our human condition, free of struggle, judgment or discontent. Not you, hanging out on a limb at the mercy of the changing phenomena that continues to fluctuate all around us. This is you at the very center of it all, a willing conscious life, accepting that *change is stability*. That change is the one thing you can be sure about; that the persistent turn of our moment to moment reality is a certainty.

CHANGE IS STABILITY

THE PURPOSE OF THESE PRACTICES is to clear the path of the debris, the negativity, tensions, toxicity, false conditioning and fears that hinders our access to the still point of ourselves, to the place of peace within. Being at the hub of the wheel of the turning world, sheltered by the sanctuary of your inner faith and trust, is perhaps the true Holy Grail. For here at the source there is Unity, and there is the Love that gives life and sustains us. And here you are not caught up in the spokes of the wheel of life that ceaselessly turns, creating change. A curious sense of the 'miraculous' may appear as the timeless, spacious qualities of your inner being become more evident, more apparent.

The work of yoga is to make the body conscious - to wake up to the sensitivity and subtlety of your body-mind and the natural peace and intelligence inherent within you. Yoga liberates the holding patterns, the suppression of tension in the body and mind from habits of disassociation and separation that can cause prolonged and needless suffering. Yoga leads you into an experience of wholeness, of unity within your-self and hence the world in which you live.

Yoga practice carries you through the portal of your body into the inner wisdom of your being that may be lying hidden or dormant. The form awakens this fundamental intelligence, cultivating a deepening awareness that nourishes and strengthens you. This process softens the armor, the tensions, the illusions which we may have falsely built within and around ourselves, to protect our bodies from what our minds could not justify, accept or understand. The ongoing practice and repetition of yoga restructures or deconstructs the memory patterns on a cellular level, as if breaking a mold to free the energy trapped within those holding patterns. For tension holds great amounts of blocked energy which when released recharges your whole system. Tension contains fuel for transformation.

EMBRACING RESISTANCE

THE DRAMA OF LIFE lies in the resistance to the feelings, thoughts and sensations that continually arise as part of living in a body with a human consciousness. The drama lives in the space *between* our attitudes and the reality of our lives. By resisting what we are, we create a dynamic, a force-field of push and pull, that confuses the easy flow of pure energy and therefore, multiplies the complexity of living. By resisting or rejecting unpleasant experiences, or holding on too firmly to experiences we do like and want, we attach ourselves to these sensations and hold ourselves hostage to them. We limit their potential growth, our potential growth, retarding the flow of energy through them which does not allow for the fulfillment of their destiny, which is to lead us somewhere new, somewhere free of the confines of attachment. To teach us something different and pertinent. To lead us to peace, freedom and happiness.

Embracing resistance is a point of faith that all will be well; the belief that essentially we live in a benevolent world, not bent on destruction yet on healing and unity. We accept there is purpose to what may appear as random and by letting life unfold without too much judgment and drama we are allowing the journey of life to reveal its hidden messages. This is really the fast lane of life, where our understanding accelerates with a rapidity that speeds up the resolution of what appear as problems. Karma, the law of cause and effect, becomes more obvious and transparent as we begin to learn quickly the effect of our actions. Our karma returns to us more swiftly, showing us ourselves and preventing prolonged hardship.

Resistance suppresses that which we do not like or want and re-enforces the condition creating layers of tension. The opposite effect of what we really want! By accepting our feelings and sensations as they unfold, we are opening the pathways to a greater freedom of expression that is not bound by the restrictions of resistance. When we embrace resistance, we are on the one hand allowing the true sensation to be experienced connecting us with its source, and on the other hand we are reducing the pain of any unpleasant feelings by not claiming them or identifying with them. We let them go and thereby de-fuse them. By embracing the sensations as they arise we allow them to flow through us like river, carrying with it any of the associated fears and tensions that dam the way to peace.

Embracing resistance does not mean that we should just sit back and allow ourselves to persist in painful situations or behavior if it is causing unbearable pain for ourselves or others. Yoga teaches us to use all our attributes to find balance by drawing on our maturing qualities of compassion, knowledge and skill.

Research into the treatment of chronic physical pain, whether that be migraines, sciatica, arthritis, child-birth or the many other symptoms of physical trauma, has shown that sufferers benefit greatly from relaxation therapy and meditations that are based on the principle of detaching from the pain by creating a observing attitude. Through exploring pain with a calm mind, breathing into the feelings, and in some techniques using visualization or internal dialogue, the association with the pain is transformed and the personal suffering subsides. We take a step back from the frontline and view our discomfort as if from a distance, objectively rather than subjectively.

A new relationship is created within the body-mind that accepts, rather than rejects, relaxing the nervous system and easing the corresponding body parts. Acceptance creates a space for change and ultimately for healing.

In essence this teaching is the dissolution of the 'I', of the ego, that can become trapped in the smaller picture of its seeming reality. When the mind opens out and ceases to identify with every sensation as being 'me', a broader perspective of vision comes into the fray, when we are bathed in the vast peace of universal consciousness that absorbs the shock of pain and soothes with the balm of enlightenment.

The promenade of small squat juniper trees leads me down the dusty hillside where I have been communing all afternoon with the sweet smell of sun-drenched alfalfa grass high up on the hills of Harbin Hot Springs. This is the ceremonial ground where our tribal Indian ancestors led their sacred medicine circles. My brown skin is wrapped in a simple white sarong, pulled comfortably through my legs and round my waist like a loin cloth. My breasts are free to merge with the intensely clean hot air. Black hair laps down my back cooling me, warding off the flies as my sandaled feet roll over the loose dry stones. My mind is a warm pasture of pleasured peace. The path changes into flatter land and the heady scent of fresh figs draws my hands up to the large black succulents that hang provocatively above me. One, two, three, maybe four I absorb into the well of my body relishing the vibrancy of their historic life. Passing over the little broken arched bridge the stream sings to me, reminding me that soon it will be dark. I tread carefully stepping over a coiled snake asleep on the woodland path and find that I am chanting 'om mahne padme hum' over and over again.

The strong pungency of sulphur comes wafting in as the sound of heavy running water reaches my ears. The baths await me in their simple temple of stone and antiquity. The worn wood decks are dotted with a few others sitting alone or in groups, their naked skin as much a part of this holy landscape as the old bay trees that shelter us. I wash off the dust and enter the sanctuary of the steaming hot mineral pool as it pours ceaselessly from deep beneath the earth's surface. It is twilight, my favorite time, when the veil between the worlds seems to open invitingly. Someone has placed fresh flowers above the mouth of the spring and candles flicker in the fading light. The small enclosure holds the energy of the space in a natural peace where no-one speaks in words, just smiles and sighs. I move slowly onto the first step down into the water and pause to breathe, the heat penetrates with an intensity that takes courage to receive. At each new step down I pause and allow my body to adjust to the seething temperature that seeks out the resistance, enticing me to accept and let go. Inch by inch I edge into this magical cauldron that melts every atom of resistance, of interference from my body and mind. I am standing up to my neck, leaning against the worn soft stone wall immersed in the power of these healing waters that quenches every part of me. I am liquid fire, burning like molten rock, dissolving the dross. After a while I wade the short distance to where the water flows in and place my head beneath its abundant baptism.

Reborn, like the phoenix, I rise up out of the fire waters and lie flat on my back on the old oak bench to cool. My skin dries instantly and I am so relaxed, purified, weightless, boundless and blissful, luxuriating in this Garden of Eden. After a while I move toward the cold pool sheltered amidst a labyrinth of trees where I submerge and re-balance my whole being. Sensational fireworks explode through me as my pores close and blood rushes to my head.

On the deck the yoga practice is beginning as the dusk holds court in the crystal clear mountain air. The emerging postures pay homage to the sanctuary of this timeless territory and we equally breathe the living and de-composing molecules of life with unreserved acceptance. My heart sculptures the syllables of this heavenly moment, resonating in feelings of gratitude and thankfulness. The body prayers move to our throat and lips which *chant the symbols of a vibrational language that bridges country and culture and sound the universal words of the soul.*

HARBIN HOT SPRINGS scintillating atmosphere, which had once been an American Indian Holy Ceremonial ground, became my home for the following year, where I studied deep body work with the inspirational Phil Caylor from the Niyama School of Healing and Massage, which put me in touch with a life-form that became the seed of my future livelihood. Harbin had then just been bought by a New York City banker who had changed his form, his life and name and was known as Ishvara. Harbin was then a rustic haven of enriching simplicity that was attracting healers and those rediscovering their lives and themselves from all over the planet. Young and old living as a community of pioneers resurrecting the true purpose of that land. It was remarkable in every respect. One day I received a soothing rhythmic healing in the warm hot spring given by Harold Dull, spontaneously creating what later became known as Watsu. Harold had come up from San Francisco where he had a Shiatsu practice and school and became a vital part of Harbins' resurrection from hippy hangout to a true sanctuary of healing.

We baked in the midday sun, covered in the soft potent natural clay we tugged from the earth around the pools and lay there like a pagan tribal ritual purifying our matter. So much immersion in the elements was food for the soul and we regularly fasted, lived on greens and fruits and prana so alive in the pure mountain air. A year of journeying through the seasons here, healing one another and restoring myself inspired me to acquire more practical wisdom which lead me to study Ayurveda with the great Dr Vasant Lad who had just arrived in the USA and was teaching his very first course at The School of Natural Medicine in Sante Fe New Mexico. Ayurveda is the medicinal, healing sister of yoga and I felt an instant affinity with this ancient teaching and practice, and blessed to have been shown such grace and synchronicity.

With a friend from Harbin we drove to New Mexico to explore that extraordinary land, stopping in sacred Taos which perhaps is one of the most artistically inspirational places on earth. We settled in Sante Fe, inhaling the pure mountain air at 7000 ft. was like drinking the finest intoxicating champagne. The seasons here are exquisitely defined by perfect temperatures, wild colors, pristine weather conditions and the harmony these natural elements bring to life. Literally golden and scarlet autumns, electric purple summer storms, pure white snow in winter and the bluest turquoise sky all year round. The immensely rich mix of Mexican, American Indian and Texan cultures creates a unique blend of art, design, food and architecture. Many healers and spiritual practitioners live in this supremely enriching environment. It is uniquely powerful and beautiful. Studying Ayurveda and learning through the ancient wisdom of Dr Vasant Lad teaching us chants to awaken our minds and leading us into Ayurvedic healing experience. I lived in a traditional adobe style house whilst having my own little art studio on the famous Canyon Road where I created and sold my batik silk dresses, kimonos and wall hangings which made for a highly creative fulfilling year abundant with incredible people and a sense of growth.

ACCEPTANCE CREATES A SPACE FOR CHANGE

ACCEPTANCE IS THE KEY ingredient in the equation of growth and transformation. Real change happens when the body and mind are in repose, in a relaxed and receptive state of being. Stillness is not the absence of movement, it is in fact a fertile and gentle environment for encouraging psychological and emotional integration.

When your energy is being consolidated and contained your senses draw inwards reversing your vision from the outside in. Stillness also alerts us to the depth of more subtle feelings which are often vibrating at such a high frequency that we need to be still in order to notice them. The outer movements of the body are on a grosser, denser level of sensation and so it naturally follows that internally the changes that occur through movement can be better reflected upon when we stop 'doing' and just 'be. Just like a boat will leave a wake as it moves through the water. So movement leaves traces in the pool of energy of your body and mind. In stillness you will be able to accept, comprehend more and feel safer to integrate new changes. Change and transformation happens on subtle, often hidden levels at first, and deep relaxation is an essential element of any yoga practice, bringing qualities of balance and healing.

It is within this still internal environment that the molecules of your psychological, emotional and physical make up have an opportunity to re-align and restructure themselves. Reflect for a moment upon the speed at which the earth rotates around the sun. You do not physically feel or see the world turning but your senses perceive the shifts in light and darkness and your body responds by adhering to the circadian cycles of night and day, affecting patterns of sleeping and waking. In fact, your whole body is vibrating at such a rate that in order to experience it you need to be very, very still.

If we had a keen vision of all that is ordinary in human life, it would be like hearing the grass grow or the squirrel's heartbeat, and we should die of that roar which is the other side of silence.

-George Elliot: Middlemarch (1872)

THE ANATOMY OF YOGA

THE DISCIPLINES OF YOGA embrace a variety of styles and modes of practice which may be asanas, (physical postures), meditative techniques, prayer or ways of living. The word 'Yoga' literally means 'to join,' 'yoke,' or 'union' and points to the purpose of practice which is to unite the body and mind bringing you into one place, at one time, thereby reducing superficial distractions, refining your focus and conscious awareness. This process is at the heart of the preservation of our sanity and food for the soul.

As the roots of yoga stem back hundreds of years its philosophy of the structure naturally carries ancient influences and traditions which add a dimension of intellectual understanding, linking you to the great lineages and rituals that enrich the quality of your practice. These teachings are still as relevant today and they were 2,0000 years ago for they delve beneath the surface of our lives to the core values that sustain our world.

Yoga has been broadly divided into four forms or four ways through which you can develop your life. Each path is complete within itself yet the inherent value of each approach serves to enrich and support the maturity of them all.

Your intention and attitude are at the pivot of how you develop within these various forms. Some people spontaneously find themselves involved in a certain path without even realizing it, yet the benefits and rewards are the same. They sublimate the ego, liberating us as part of the greater whole from suffering, on the path to enlightenment.

Here is a very brief breakdown of these paths to layout the basic map and structure of yogic philosophy.

THE FOUR PATHS OF YOGA

THE FIRST FORM IS KARMA YOGA, the path of Action which ideally cultivates qualities of generosity and unselfishness. You can practice Karma Yoga by focusing your work and activities on benefiting others happiness and fulfillment. Working in a directly activist role such as through charity, or teaching, or caring for others who are needy, deprived or sick are ways through which we can cultivate 'good karma' These selfless actions can cleanse the mind of greed, jealousy, hatred and egoism whether they be charitably offered or as part of your livelihood. Karma is the law of cause and effect where everything we do or say returns to us in one form or another.

BHAKTI YOGA IS THE PATH OF DEVOTION which is traditionally practiced through consistent unconditional love and care whether this be to your husband/wife, a friend, a family member or a teacher. Traditionally Bhakti Yoga was primarily associated with the devotion a disciple has to his or her spiritual teacher. This path develops qualities of empathy, commitment, loyalty and compassion, cleansing the mind of superficial gratification and constant craving after new thrills and relationships.

GYANA YOGA IS THE PATH OF KNOWLEDGE which develops the mind of reason, will and intellect through studying the philosophical and scientific texts on yoga. However, study of any pure spiritual, philosophical or religious texts also serves to refine and enrich the intellect. This is scholastic training which removes ignorance, dullness, judgment and assumptions from the mind.

RAJA YOGA IS THE SCIENCE of mental control which steadies the mind, developing increased focus, concentration, self-reflection and meditative skills. To cultivate these qualities Raja Yoga is then divided into three subdivisions which actually defines how yoga is most commonly practiced in our western society. These subdivisions all contribute to the aim of Raja

Yoga which is to experience an elevated, yet deeply rooted state of consciousness known as *Samadhi*.

THE SUBDIVISIONS OF RAJA YOGA

MANTRA YOGA is the repetition of certain sounds, syllables or sacred names that are verbally spoken, chanted or repeated silently. Mantra yoga focuses the mind, clearing the chit chat from the foreground of our thinking and generating a healing vibration of sound and association. This reverberates throughout and whole body creating a dynamic energy imbued with clarity and harmony. Mantra yoga is practiced within many eastern spiritual traditions as well as Buddhism.

HATHA YOGA gives attention primarily to the physical body in order to relax, detox, align and strengthen the form so that the mind can become quiet and focused. Hatha yoga integrates asanas (postures) and pranayama (breathing techniques) which constitute two of the most vital ingredients that balance the energy systems of the body, from the muscles and bones to the organs, nervous system, endocrine system, lymphatic system, circulation and respiration. Practice keeps the body in a healthy and youthful state of being. Most styles of yoga such as Iyengar and Ashtanga yoga come under this banner. Today teachers tend to fuse different styles together so names such as Power Yoga or Dynamic Yoga are more common yet they usually come into this category.

KUNDALINI YOGA, the third mode, works directly with the coil of transformative energy, symbolically represented as a serpent, most often lying asleep or dormant at the base of the spine. Kundalini energy is awakened through specific use of postures, breathing and concentration that stimulates the benefits found in Hatha yoga. Kundalini Yoga uses Breath of Fire, mantra and meditation within specific asanas to liberate this energy. In the west we have been mostly influenced by Yogi Bhajans, 3Ho 'Happy Healthy Holy Organization' of mainly Sikhs who teach these techniques. Practice is powerfully de-toxing and accelerates the elimination process through the endocrine system, boosting the immune system.

TANTRA YOGA, also known as Maha Yoga, is a combination of the four main paths of yoga as described above. Tantra Yoga focuses on the cultivation and circulation of subtle energy through the seven predominant Chakras, which loosely described, are a system of vortexes of dynamic subtle energy that relate to our physical, psychological and emotional wellbeing. They are connected through the many portals of the physical body including the function of the seven key endocrine glands. Practice works specifically on the transformation of sexual and raw creative energy as an intense and rare path to liberation.

Tantra Yoga is most effectively practiced with a partner as a pathway to experience a divine loving unity on all levels of consciousness and the bliss of Samadhi

THE EIGHT LIMBS OF YOGA

Each of the forms of Raja Yoga are defined by the same eight attributes known as the *eight limbs of yoga* (Ashtanga). Ashtanga means to purify the mind through these eight steps which are aspects of Hatha in all its many forms, Kundalini, Mantra or Tantra Yoga.

YAMA refers to control and relates to psychological purification through awareness of moral and social issues. This includes developing qualities on honesty, truthfulness, nonviolence, forbearance, kindness, sexual continence, eating moderately, and cleansing the body.

NIYAMA refers to Rules of Conduct and relates to leading a contemplative lifestyle, developing qualities of contentment, modesty and discretion. Practice includes prayer, study of spiritual teachings, belief in God and self-discipline.

ASANAS refers to Postures and relates to the practice of physical yoga postures to calm the body and bring stillness to the mind as a preparation for meditation.

PRANAYAMA refers to Control of Breath and relates to the practice of breathing techniques, and the practice of Bandhas, muscular control.

PRATHYAHARA refers to Withdrawal of Sensory Perceptions that utilizes Kundalini Yoga techniques that suspend the breath, holding the mind and thereby absorbing the senses. This cultivates the ability to reflect inwardly.

DHARANA refers to Concentration and cultivates the ability to become deeply absorbed and focused on subtle energy through the Chakra system and Mantra practice. Sensory Awareness Meditation supports this process.

DHYANA refers to Uninterrupted Meditation where the 'I', or the ego is dissolved into the greater consciousness, into a continuity of unbroken awareness.

SAMADHI refers to an experience of Transcendental Peace where equilibrium, total joy, deep peace and complete awareness absorb ones whole being in a pure state of consciousness. Samadhi is considered a supreme divine state of being that changes our body chemistry and therefore emotional and psychological patterning on every level. When a long period of Samadhi is attained it is not considered necessary to practice other forms of yoga any more, as the transformation is complete and becomes an ongoing reality.

VIPASSANA INSIGHT RETREAT

One instant is eternity
Eternity is the now
When you see through this one instant
You see through the one who sees.

- Wu-Men
(1183-1260)

I am in the laboratory. In the laboratory of my mind; in the cauldron of the creation of myself unfolding in consciousness moment by moment. Like petals of a water lily opening out from the center in a continuous flow, without ceasing. I am the laboratory. I am in the midst of' becoming'. I can feel the unfolding of my existence rippling outwards forming my ongoing living presence. So softly. So peacefully. This is blissful. It feels like the 'love to live' To endlessly live. Is this love? 'To be' forever. I am even beyond my breath, beyond the impulse to breathe; I am before my breath.. as though my breath has stopped and I am suspended in space, completely free, rendered weightless, formless.

I am the open space, a pure space, a neutral space that contains what I call 'myself.' I am the space. How vast!

There are no boundaries here, no definition or edge that could entrap my mind or limit me, no notions that catch my breath. Simply an endless continuity of awareness unbroken by physical moorings. Uninterrupted by the need for change, or longing or anticipation. Unencumbered by pain or discomfort. I am simply conscious of being conscious. Being consciousness. The sweetness of this bliss pours over me. This is nectar. What bliss in this place. I am solid yet not. I am here yet not. There is no duality yet neither is there singularity. Just open vast limitless peace.

Suddenly, my body begins to vibrate at an incredible rate, there is a sharp pulling pain in my ankles as if I am being dragged out of myself through my feet. A loud whooshing sound echoes from somewhere but I cannot tell if it is from within me or outside of me. And I am spinning, spinning faster and faster. Then just as suddenly I find myself suspended in the huge kitchen watching a busy scene of all the cooks preparing food. I recognize someone I know and smile at her, but she does not see me. No-one sees me. I am up above, in the air looking down on it all. They are cooking sautéed tofu and rice. Big bowls of salad sit on the counters. The colors are extraordinarily vivid, like technicolor, and the sounds of pots and plates seem different somehow as if the noise is being played through a loud speaker in a cave echoing inside me. I am outside now and a dog is barking sharply. I know it has seen me. I am hovering over the lawn looking down at the dog looking at me! I am swept up across the rooftop to the other side of the building and I hear a very loud bang, like a door being slammed and I am lying frozen on the floor curled up like a foetus. I have fallen forward off my zafu. The hall is empty, all the others have gone to dinner.

Gradually I collect my body, slowly stand and feel my breath come pouring in. The darkness is bright with tiny molecules of scintillating light like a fine meteor shower slowly descending upon me. I am light, very light, almost too light and can hardly feel the solidity beneath my feet. Am I too light to walk ? Would it be easier to fly? I laugh at my thought and that helps me solidify. 'Just place one foot in front of the other, step by step you can move', I coax myself. It's easy. I feel as though I am on a conveyor belt being carried along by some unseen force, so smoothly, so gracefully, I am smiling, smiling inside.

The aroma of basmati rice, soya sauce and tofu waft towards me as I enter the large dining room. I know already what we are having for dinner! it is one of my favorites. Eating is such a pleasure, such a joy. Every bite bursts into a million flavors totally absorbing me, my sensory awareness, they become my consciousness. Joy seeps through every pore of my being and I am grateful, I am happy, I am fulfilled.

Vipassana, Insight Meditation, turned up quite unexpectedly, like all the best things in life. Word had spread through the Maui Zendo where I lived, that a retreat was being held at Akahi Farms, just down the road, and the teacher Anagarika Munindra would be present there for 10 days. I knew very little about Vipassana meditation but my thirst for more experience and knowledge drew me to it like a duck to water. My training so far had been within the rigorous, and crisp style of Soto Zen and I had heard that Vipassana offered a more compassionate path of contemplation that intrigued me.

It would be lacking somehow, if I were to talk about my first Vipassana retreat without mentioning Joseph. Though not directly relevant he stands as an essential ingredient marking my memory there and I want to pay tribute to this beautiful soul who I joined with in spirit and love. I have learnt that people come into our lives to reflect us in some way, manifesting as an embodiment of an energy that we are being asked to respond to; to embrace in one way or another as an extension of ourselves.

Vipassana transpired to be one of the greatest methods for meditation I have so far encountered. I fell totally into it, sitting close to the teacher, absorbing every word of guidance from Anagarika Munindra, with a disciplined embrace. Joe, however, slouched around at the back of the room, unable to sit upright for the long periods of meditation, and was sometimes missing altogether. I was used to all those hours of concentration as I had been at the Zendo for many years already, and I felt for him. I began to sense deep levels of suffering coming from his body and mind and was surprised to find myself being more endeared to him because of it! This was new to me as I had become quite a purist over the years but had connected with him in such a way that I strongly empathized with his pain. As the retreat went on we learnt *Metta*, the Practice of Loving Kindness which also altered how I related to pain, mine as well as other peoples'

Vipassana engaged my mind in a process that brought my focus into a mental stance of self-inquiry. Like an open question. As if I had an ongoing 'question mark' poised unmoving at the pivot of my attention. I was looking with interest, with curiosity at the breath and the internal processes as they occurred. It brought me unequivocally into the moment. Into the Here and Now. Vipassana is a deeply refreshing, enlivening and dynamic practice that naturally embraced all aspects of my humanity, of my human condition. The practice gave me a tool, like a discerning microscope through which I could closely observe the internal mechanism of my physical body, emotional impulses and thought processes. A totally fascinating experience.

The notation process of Vipassana goes through progressive stages of concentration beginning with observing, feeling and noting the 'rising and falling' of the breath. This stage is at the very core of the practice and sustains the development of the meditation as one's awareness engages with the many other aspects of your conscious awareness. The practice moves onto further notation, of mentally 'naming', identifying physical feelings and all the subtle senses. Touching, hearing, smelling, tasting, thinking, dreaming, imagining, walking, sensations of all kinds whether emotional, psychological or sensory.

As my concentration became more consistent, more intimate, the universe within me began to open out, unfolding new yet familiar parts of myself. My perceptions were changing and gave rise to fresh insights into the origins of feelings and thoughts. Unexpected aspects of the body and mind revealed themselves shedding light where there had been darkness. One day as I practice an image arises in my mind.

Seeing, Seeing, Seeing? Notes my inquiring mind. I am seeing a dark red oblong shape with a white edge that looks soft and moist. Tiny fine fibers stick up on the surface of the shape. The image seems large, very large, as if I am looking at a cinema screen. What is it? The only way to observe it is to maintain an inquiring focus. Seeing, Seeing? Not assuming, not examining. Just allowing this sight to be there, looking closely but not identified with it. For what seems a very long time I am seeing this. The image grows enormous filling my inner vision when suddenly, as if I knew all along, I know what I am seeing. It is the inside of my body, my skin, the hair follicles, the muscle and tissue. The very second I realize this I am going into it, becoming it, like deep sea diving I am in the throbbing interior of my flesh. There is a pulsation and I see a very tiny egg shaped light that has an almost imperceptible black line across the middle of it. Seeing? Seeing? I know it. It is a cell. A blood cell. I recognize it and I am that pulsating cell.

Some more months passed by and I eventually left the island, The Maui Zendo and my lofty Eucalyptus grove hut for Massachusetts to join the long winter retreat at The Insight Meditation Society in Barre.

Over one hundred people participated in this three month retreat and we were all fortunate enough to receive the teachings and guidance of Jack Kornfield, Joseph Goldstein, Sharon Saltzberg and Anagarika Munindra. They were a remarkable team who lead us skillfully and admirably into this sacred territory with compassion and light-heartedness. For me the guidance of Jack and Sharon has stayed clearly in my mind and heart. Sharon was an inspiration through the practice of Metta, and Jacks' deeply poetic and transparent mind shone through all his communication.

With no communication at all to other practitioners or with the outside world; no letters, no calls; no shopping or leaving the center, it was a pristine opportunity for cultivating and deepening one's meditation practice. The center had once been a Benedictine Monastery and it was beautifully situated amongst many trees and lakes.

I will always be grateful for the blessing of that time and the exceptional quality of care that was given by all.

Five sittings, that must be four hours of time, I make my way to the front door. Opening it warm earthy scent floats through me and I am gone; I have disappeared. I am the red and golden bursting light that floods the autumn trees. I am the radiant orange sun glowing up above. I am the soft breeze moving, and I am the leaves rustling. I have vanished, yet remain in everything. I am dissolved in total empathy with what I see, smell, hear, sense. The world becomes me and there is joy.

There were three days left of the retreat and our silence was to be broken in stages. The first allocated time for talking with those I had sat with for 3 months was for half an hour after lunch. Now, writing this, I cannot help laughing at the surge of energy that came with my first words, as if I had not spoken for ten years. I felt like I had suddenly arrived on a different planet! The din in the dining room was overwhelming and my nervous system felt highly peeked at the dynamic that such close encounters with others elicited. I then understood why our silence was better broken bit by bit as it would have been simply too much to launch into open-ended conversation. But I will never forget that first discussion with a guy who, believe or not, was from my home town in England! He was an artist who mainly painted Buddha's and did this retreat every year as a source of valuable inspiration. I, like many others there, had powerful insights, awesome inner visions and transcendent experiences that had enriched my soul.

Deep in the night I walk down the dark staircase meeting one or two other souls savoring the moonlight. The moon beams soften the royal blue atmosphere creating a fitting cloak for my wakeful spirit. Sleeping was no longer sleep as I had come to know it. When I lay down it was simply to rest my body for a while as my mind was already rested, deeply rested and at peace. Finding my place in the empty meditation hall I sit comfortably on my zafu. The room is still and dark and cool. I drape my shawl around me and close my eyes. Peace, presence- I am crystal clear and there is joy laughing inside me. My spine feels very strong, very straight, connected to the earth beneath and open to the space above. I am hearing, I am breathing, I am sensing. I am here.

A warm liquid vibration is circulating at the base of my spine and I am seeing a black silvery lake. There is a rippling sensation that I feel and see and out of the lake appears a radiant white lotus, perfect in form and color, sharp and powerful against the glistening black water. Opening wider and wider it rises up out of the lake and I see it has a long green thick curving stem. The White Lotus begins to look tinged with pink and I see that the stem is in fact a Serpent, coiling up out of the lake carrying the lotus on its head. It is so beautiful, so majestic and I am vibrating, my whole spine is shaking as I feel and see the serpent lift the lotus higher and higher up out of the hidden depths, up my spine. The sensation within me is ecstatic and I am laughing inside, and then there is a flash of light. Clear white light. The lotus has filled my mind. My consciousness is illuminated and I am completely Awake. More awake than I have ever been.

Birds are singing as I open my eyes in the dawn of a new day. I slowly rise and bring my hands together in prayer mudra. Gassho. I bow to the west, to the east, to the north and to the south. I bow to my zafu and walk out to satisfy the hunger in my belly. Breakfast will soon be served.

Vipassana took me on a journey I could not have imagined and by the end of the retreat I wanted to ordain as a Buddhist nun, but when I asked Munindra about this he laughed at me and said, "Ah, Jacqualine, you are many things, but one thing you are not is a nun! You have much to do in the world as you are." I was quite surprised and somewhat disappointed but decided to stay on at IMS anyway as a scholarship had been offered to me to meditate there which would cover my basic expenses of food and accommodation plus a little extra. However, after another month the snow was thick on the ground, the wind blew strong and I felt terribly cold. Only a handful of people remained at the center and the remaining few occupied a small wing of the building that was drafty and dark, so I returned to the Pacific island of Maui to warm up, paint silk, frequent the zendo and meet old friends.

Vipassana and Metta Bhavana originate from the Theravadan tradition of Buddhist practice. Vipassana means 'Insight' and one can say reflects the male, yang aspect of our nature. It is investigative, inquiring and assertive, yet contains within it a foundation of receptivity; a foundation of Acceptance that supports the natural arising of our neurosis, the condition of our duality.

What I found in these practices were the tools with which I could go into the laboratory of my body, mind and heart and observe the nature of my inner states of being. After that first retreat I felt as though I had drunk long and deep from an immense pool of wisdom that saturated every aspect of my being. There was no corner of myself that had been 'left out' or excluded. There had been an acknowledgement of thought processes, feelings, sensations and imagination. I felt complete and sustained.

THE INQUIRING MIND MEDITATION

The process and the goal are not separate; they are one.

-Mahatma Gandhi

The following meditation is at the very core of Vipassana practice and serves to gently anchor your concentration to deepen the pathways to peace and equanimity. Developing a shift in focus appropriate for cultivating a meditative awareness can be a life-times work, so do not be disheartened when you find your mind wandering here and there. We are so often educated to be goal oriented and encouraged to focus on the result rather than the actual process of getting there. The *arriving* rather than the *journey*. Within meditation it is quite the reverse. The process is the goal! In fact, the process and the goal are not separate, they are one.

Meditation is a timeless practice, a path within itself that only exists in the moment. You can only be where you are which naturally contains all you need to be at that moment. The purpose of meditation is to bring you into the heart of the moment and heal the disassociation of the fragmented, dualistic, striving mind. To 'be here now' as Ram Dass so succinctly put it. For it is by being yourself, in the moment, in this non-judgmental way that you become intimate and familiar with parts of yourself that yearn to be recognized, that may have been submerged, forgotten, ignored or depressed. Being in the moment helps you to feel whole and grounded where a spontaneous sense of satisfaction arises, as if you have had a long satisfying drink after days parched walking through the desert.

Often what prevents us from being in the moment is that we are habitually and unconsciously predicting what will happen based on past conditioning. This can lead us away from the pure potential of the moment and influence or even limit the actual experience. Our minds are jumping ahead to the possible result of a situation or feeling which we are probably completely unaware of. Insight Meditation serves to unwind the habitual assumptions, expectations and predictions we are unconsciously making so that we can develop deeper and clearer insight into our motivation, behavior and other personality traits. This process of slowing down our reactionary responses and replacing them with insight and awareness brings us into the laboratory of our mind, where we feel directly in touch with the forming of feelings and thoughts; their origins, associations and attachments. It is an exciting, pro-active yet peaceful experience that I can compare with no other. The results speak for themselves and each one of us will discover unique and relevant insights that can bring much joy and resolution.

During meditation you will find that your attention often wanders away and you can lose your concentration. Strong feelings, whether physical, emotional or psychological will also arise to be noticed that may temporarily take you away from the 'Rising and 'Falling' of your breath. This is a natural phenomenon which Vipassanna meditation embraces and in fact utilizes as part of the practice of developing insight. For instance, if you begin to feel a sharp pain in your knee, rather than try to ignore the pain or identify with it by thinking 'Oh my knee hurts', we simply observe the feeling of the pain with the same inquiring mind as we do the breath. We embrace the experience of discomfort, observing it with a peaceful mind thinking 'Pain? Pain' just as we did 'Rising? and Falling?'

By noticing the pain with interest and inquiry, breathing consciousness into it, we actually take the sting of it! It is really quite miraculous as the first thing you will notice is that the feeling is not as bad as you had thought it was. By placing your undivided attention there in a detached and inquiring way your 'acceptance' diffuses it and on some very primary level, acts like an anesthetic. The inquiring, detachment of your mind goes beyond the periphery of the pain and beneath the surface where there is a sense of ease.

When we stop identifying with feelings as being a fixed part of ourselves, or belonging to us, we give those feelings less reason to be there! For it is our *relationship* to an experience that decides how it will affect us, not the feeling itself. By changing our relationship to pain we transform the actual sensation of it within us and open up news pathways of association that directly affects the nervous system and therefore its physical reality. The signals then coming to the brain change and our psychological perception expands into a greater field of awareness where our insights arise. This same inquiring relationship is then applied to whatever feelings or sensations come to the foreground of your meditation practice.

Simply by following this practice you will be bringing yourself into the subtle environment of your inner life and therefore being in the lap of the moment, at the center of yourself, wherever that may be. Here you will discover a place of safety and refuge just waiting for you to open the door and awaken into the full potential of your consciousness. Be assured that the quality of your concentration will change over time. As the word 'practice' implies, meditation is just that! It is the ongoing consistency of repeating the meditation daily that naturally hones the craft of your practice and enables your presence to develop. The peace of the temple you seek is already there within you. Be still, breathe and simply practice being there.

Begin with a 20 minute session and eventually build up to one hour at a time.

INSIGHT MEDITATION PRACTICE

Bring your mind to focus softly
On the rise and fall of your breath.
On the rise of your abdomen as you inhale
And on the fall of your abdomen as you exhale
Concentrate lightheartedly as the breath is subtle
Focus softly, no pressure, no hurry.
Your abdomen rising and falling.

As you feel your breath flow in and out
Focus your mind with a sense of inquiry.
As if you are asking your breath a question?
An open question
Let your mind be lighthearted,
Observing, inquiring.

With an open question in your mind
Follow the feeling, the sensation of your breath.
Watching where the breath goes, how it flows
Take an interest in the passage of your breath.
As you inhale let your mind follow the sensation of your breath
Inquiring into its passage?
Feeling the breath flow in, your abdomen rises
In your mind note 'Rising'?
As you exhale, feel the breath begin to flow out
Your abdomen falling
And mentally note with an inquiring,
Curious mind 'Falling'?
Becoming more intimate with the journey of your breath

Become aware of the very beginning of the inhalation – Rising?
To the middle of the breath
To the fullness of the whole inhalation.
Then staying very close with your full attention
Feel the very beginning of the exhalation - Falling?
As you feel the impulse of the breath leaving your body
Through to the middle of the exhalation
To the emptiness of no breath.

Be conscious of this emptiness
Then again feel that impulse to begin inhaling
Staying very close to the passage of it - Rising?
Through the middle of its passage to the full breath.
Then as the impulse to exhale begins – Falling?
Through the middle to the complete feeling of no breath.
Emptiness

Watch the breath closely like a mother watches a child
With love and attention, compassionately.
If your mind wanders
As soon as you realize this
Note 'wandering'? Wandering?
And bring yourself back to your inquiring mind
Observing your breath with interest
Rising? ∾ Falling? ∾
Rising ∾ Falling ∾

THE BODY OF BREATH

When the doors of perception are cleansed all things are seen as being infinite.

-Aldous Huxley

Pranayama harmonizes and balances the flow of prana within you. It is the conscious control of breathing, through techniques, which focus on the nadi and chakra systems. The following practices are ones which I love and have taught to many people. The instant dynamic of these techniques give transforming results. Like all things the more familiar you are with them, the easier they are to do and the more effective they become. Your ability and receptivity will increase. Even though your nadis may be 'out of action,' your sinuses blocked or your lungs weak, the repetition of pranayama will gradually clear the pranic pathways, strengthening the corresponding physical elements that naturally empower your breathing.

After practicing some of these techniques you may sense tingling sensations at the extremities of your hands, feet and head or even feel quite light-headed. This is natural. When you begin to intake greater amounts of oxygen and prana it causes the blood cells to dilate and recharge. This influx of energy stimulates the body to release excess toxicity and built up tensions. This process causes the blood cells to divide and separate which recharges your bio-chemistry to manufacture clean blood now imbued with fresh oxygen and prana. The higher ratio of these elements in your blood stimulates your system to vibrate and buzz. During sleep or deep relaxation your blood cells also divide and regenerate which helps to rebuild your metabolism, restoring energy, strengthening tissue and calming the nervous system. This naturally empowers all the connective tissue to function better which informs the muscles that all is well and tension is released. But the conscious practice of pranayama influences more subtle dimensions of your body-mind reality, opening the chakras to inform and inspire your awareness of the formless spirit of your being.

Practice will undoubtedly make you more aware of your breathing in general, and therefore enrich your insight into life. You will automatically feel uplifted, relaxed and centered. This is food for the soul.

PURE CONNECTED BREATH – *unwinding* – *'simply breathe breath'*

The purpose of *connected breathing* is to link your mind up with the sensations of breathing and nourish your 'abdominal brain' in the hara. It puts you in touch with the physical passage of your breath and engages your mind in the process. I have found connected breathing very helpful at the start of a yoga session to help to slow down the brain waves and bring your consciousness into the body and into the moment. The process will also reduce feelings of anxiety and panic or asthma attacks. Asthma is a condition where the exhalation is shortened which in turn reduces the intake of breath and oxygen. Connected breathing helps to balance this condition.

This breathing pattern is best practiced either lying down or sitting, but you can be in any position. It is helpful though for your spine to be aligned and straight if possible, and if not then be as you are.

The Practice

Through the nose simply breathe in to the count of four and exhale to the count of four.

Feel *the sensation of your breath as it flows into the body. Let the breath flow down to the hara as deeply as possible (abdomen)*

*And then exhale **feeling** the breath flow out*

Focus your mind on counting the breath as you inhale, and counting the breath on the exhale.

Practice this for a few minutes then pause and reflect on the sensations within you.

When the capacity of your hara to take in more air expands you can increase the length of your inhalation and exhalation to a maximum of eight. So it would be breathe in the count of 8 and breathe out to the count of 8.

This practice is not meant to be a great effort. Monitor your ability and breathe in a relaxed way without forcing your lungs. Some people may find even four counts in and out too much. If so, begin with two or three and build up.

There is no hurry - take your time.

YOGIC BREATH – *Opening - 'total immersion breath'*

The purpose of this practice is to exercise the full capacity of your lungs, diaphragm and abdomen. This breath also nourishes the three most powerful nerve centers; the *pelvic plexus* in your abdomen, *the solar plexus* between your ribs and the *cardiac plexus* around your heart. I have used this practice to initiate and complete a yoga session, before deep relaxation, Savasanna - corpse pose.

The Practice

Very slowly breathe into the abdomen, pushing your hara out.
As you breathe in then allow your diaphragm to fill up -
you will feel your ribs being stretched to the sides

Continue to breathe in filling the upper lung
allowing your chest to expand
let your shoulders go back

Now slowly exhale
controlling the release of the breath through your nose
from the hara first, then from the lungs
and finally the chest
Pause on empty in repose
reflect inwardly on how you feel
and begin the process again.
Practice this three times
then relax

MULABHANDA – *Root Lock*

Mulabhanda refers to the locking of the root chakra, Muladhara, and is the key Bhanda used in Kundalini yoga which can be integrated into other yoga forms to strengthen, stabilize and absorb Shakti. The technique involves squeezing the perineum and anal sphincter for men and in women squeezing the vaginal walls. This creates a strong pelvic floor. The navel is also drawn inwards with the breath, and up towards the solar plexus. This internal hold strengthens the roots of your spine and harnesses the nature of the root chakra so that energy is not lost, drawing the vital transformative kundalini power upwards. It closes this opening in the lower part of the body so that there is no leakage of the transformative potential you have generated through Khapalbhati.

ANTARA AND BHAYA KUMBHAKA
BREATH – *Balancing Purifying Breath*

Kumbhaka breath is at the heart of Hatha yoga practice and the purpose of support conscious connection and transformation to the body mind. Practice also serves to draw out impurities from the lungs and abdomen, which also helps to eliminate toxins from the internal organs, cleansing the body of stale air, excess carbon dioxide and static digestive energy. As more oxygen is absorbed this helps to improve the flow of prana into these systems. Mulabhanda (root lock) as described later in this chapter seals the practice.

The Practice

Slowly breathe into your hara and solar plexus
expanding your diaphragm for the count of six
and squeeze the ribs into the lungs
whilst drawing in Root Lock, Mulabhanda
Hold the breath like this for 3 seconds
then slowly exhale releasing Root Lock
till you are empty to create an emptiness there for a few seconds

Then practice a few natural breaths

Repeat the process between three to six times.
Then just soften your breath and belly and tune in to how your
feel.

POLARITY BREATH – *Gravity Levity Breath*

The purpose of the Polarity Breath is to align your awareness with the forces of gravity and levity creating a sense of stability. The magnetic energy and pull of the earth beneath you, keeps you grounded in the root chakra and centered in the hara, whereas the forces above you keep you upright with the potential for spiritual insight and experience. You are the bridge between density and light; between the finite and infinite.

To benefit from this practice sit in a cross-legged or lotus position or kneeling, with or without a cushion. This is an excellent centering practice before meditation or simply practiced whenever you feel out of touch with your body or too caught up in your mind.

The Practice

Inhale deeply as if into the base of your spine
Hold the breath there for a few seconds letting a pressure build
Then imagine a root extends from the base of your spine to the
centre of the Earth

Exhale down that root, the breath flowing down beneath you.
Become aware of the pull of gravity, the magnetism,
the density and stability holding you down.
Then, maintaining that awareness of your connection to the earth

Inhale into the diaphragm holding the breath there.
Imagine there is a fountain of light above your head
Exhale up into that fountain way above your head
into the spaciousness above and beyond you.

Let the light shower down around you returning to the Earth.
Now just sit in that Polarity
In that awareness of
stability beneath you
and spaciousness above your head.

TRADITIONAL PRANAYAMA – *Alternate breaths – 'brain balancer'*

Pranayama regulates the flow of prana directly up into the right and left hemispheres of the brain, calming your central nervous system and clearing your mind. Practice also helps to balance and open Ajna, the sixth chakra, the third eye of insight, psychic awareness and spiritual awakening.

By separating out the nasal passages your body temperature is also modified through *ida* and *pingali nadi* that help to regulate body heat and cold. For those who find their sinuses become blocked easily or are prone to headaches this is an excellent antidote. You can use this any time as a way of preparing your mind for study, or meditation, before sleep, when you wake up or as part of a yoga session. Pranayama is a powerful medicine to heal feelings of separation and isolation. You will build up the retention of the breath as your lungs develop. Take it easy. Go slowly. Best practiced sitting upright, or if not possible you can recline. Clear your nose by blowing first.

Traditionally men use their right hand to control the nasal passage, and women their left. Using the right hand balances the left side of the brain (conceptual/structural mind), and the left hand balances the right brain (imaginative/abstract mind).

The Practice

Breathing in lift your hand to the nose
Close the outside nostril with your thumb
Place the middle finger between the eyebrow
pushing up slightly on the skin
and then exhale through the open nostril

Now breathe in through the open side
taking the breath into the hara (abdomen)
then close that nostril off will your fourth finger
so that both side are closed

Hold the breath for 4 counts (you can build up very gradually to
21 counts)
Your eyes are closed and you are looking inwards and up
into the center of your forehead (the third eye point)
where your attention naturally gathers.
Then release the opposite nostril and slowly exhale
Pause on empty - reflecting inwardly.

Now breathe in through that open nostril all they way into the
hara.
Then close it off and count following the directions as above.
Now release the opposite and exhale.
Continue in this way for 6 rounds to begin with.

Meditate, relax and enjoy your inner space of clarity and balance.

LONGEVITY BREATH - *for stillness and consciousness*

Yogic philosophy reveals that the yogi does not measure life in years, but in breaths. That the ageing process of the body is restrained by slowing down the natural flow of breathing and reducing how often you breathe. Stories of experienced practitioners of yoga often sight their ability to remain under water for long periods of time, having first filled their lungs with breath to a huge capacity and then completely slowing down the exhalation, which I must add is not recommended without many years of experience and the presence of a teacher.

Images of snakes, such as the *caduceus* or *kundalini*, are often used as symbols of immortality, healing or life energy because they breathe once every five minutes, thereby prolonging their lives, some snakes living to a hundred years or more. The same principle applies to the turtle and tortoise, which are also used as symbols of ancient wisdom and long life in south pacific cultures.

Practicing this breath not only expands your lungs, but also strengthens your ability to retain the breath and control the exhalation. As we have noted the *release* of the breath is even more important than the inhalation. Exhalation slows down the rhythms of the body, directly regulating your heart-beat and calming the central nervous system. The process engages your mind in the experience of letting go with a profound sense of self awareness. The purpose of this breath is to help you enjoy a long and healthy life.

This is a wonderful breath to include at the beginning of a yoga session or before meditation, sleep or to reduce feelings of anxiety. You can practice lying down or sitting with a straight spine.

The Practice

Breathe in slowly to the count of five
slowly filling your abdomen and lungs
holding the breath deep inside
to the count of seven
then begin to exhale through the nostrils
making sure your mouth is completely closed
to the count of eight
Letting your mind follow the passage
of your exhalation instant by instant.
Pause on completion of the exhalation
reflecting inwardly on the sensations -
without moving
until you feel still inside
and repeat these rounds from six to twenty times.

DOUBLE FOUNTAIN BREATH - *liberating –*
'complete chill out breath'

The purpose of this technique is to connect up three vital power centers of your body that enhance the circulation and expansion of your pranic energy. This practice cultivates a link between your *abdominal brain*, with the power and wisdom of the *heart chakra*, and the pranic doorway in the *crown of your head*. Double Breaths integrate your emotions, increasing absorption of any undigested feelings and releases surplus energy to be regenerated. This breath is also shown as part of Tantric Breathing later in the book.

This is an excellent practice to include as part of your meditation practice or to complete a yoga session. During meditation, psychological and emotional tensions can build up, weakening your concentration and focus. Practicing the double breaths will effectively change your inner dynamic, transforming density into light. Try one double breath at a time. Always pause after completing as the flow of upward drawing prana needs time to complete its cycle. You will feel it. Just let it happen. Use this breath with discretion. Enjoy…

The Practice

Breathe deeply into the heart and upper lung
holding the breath there for 5 seconds
gently pushing your shoulders back

Then exhale half of the breath
and directly inhale again
all the way into your hara
holding the breath there for another 5 seconds

Now slowly exhale
visualising the breath flowing through the crown of
your head like a fountain above you
.....way above your head
 roll your eyes under closed eye lids
looking upwards and inwards to the centre of your forehead
where your attention naturally gathers
as the breath flows out through the crown of your head
imagine it falling back down all around you
to your feet
then just bathe in that experience
just observe how you feel without trying
to change it

BREATH OF FIRE – *Khapalbhati*

Breath of Fire is the predominant breath used in
Kundalini Yoga and powerfully boosts the bodies'
metabolism, detoxifying and strengthening internal
organs and viscera. The rapidity and force within the

technique sends oxygen and prana rich blood to the brain dilating the blood cells and recharging the nervous system which is then able to let go and calms deeply in repose. The blood cells are stimulated to divide and multiply totally regenerating your system. The dynamic wheels of the chakras are spun allowing for any blocked energy to be released bringing the whole psycho-physiological system into a renewed state of being.

The practice involves a sharp exhale through the nostrils, as if you were blowing your nose, and a deep yet soft inhalation to the solar plexus and hara, your lower diaphragm. In Kundalini yoga Breath of Fire is integrated into many different asanas and practices but is also carried out just by itself and as an instrumental way to prepare for meditation.

During the practice close your eyes and focus the mind inwards and upwards towards Ajna, the third eye chakra at the center of your forehead. You can physically draw the eyes upwards towards this area. This allows for the conscious direction of prana to the higher mind and opens the doorway of insight and a sense of transcendence. An altered state of awareness.

As the sensations of Breath of Fire create intense vibrations and sensations throughout the body-mind post any practice, it is of great importance to allow for integration, stillness and reflection as part of the practice which is held in place through Bhandas.

Khapalbhati always completes with a Bhanda, a lock, which is a holding and squeezing of various internal muscles with control of the breath to harness the prana allowing for the balanced integration that breath of fire creates. There are a few Bhandas carried out to internalize and integrate energy from different Khapalbhati asanas. Mulabhanda is very important post breath of fire to stabilize the intense flow of Shakti, vital energy, in the direction of your heart chakra, Anahata and Ajna the third eye chakra conscious awareness.

BREATH ATTUNEMENT

The Breath is the Bridge between your body and your mind.

WHEN YOU OBSERVE the tide of the breath with interest and receptivity you create a bridge over which insights can pass. Breathing is the only involuntary function that you can voluntarily control and has the unique position of being the one element that begins our conscious life, and that ends it. With our first breath we are born and with our last, we pass away. The breath is the continuous thread that contains the traces of our hidden memory and the patterns of our unfolding lives as each breath is born from the last.

As your awareness becomes anchored in observing the breath your Attention becomes food for growth, fostering change and transformation allowing your body to deeply relax. This nourishes your self-awareness, bringing to fruition and completion the cycle of old patterns that may be causing feelings of pain, limitation or discomfort in all aspects of your being. Sensations, fears, trauma and stories stored in the landscape of your body/mind, of your psycho-physiology and cellular make-up arise to be noticed. These arising internal experiences receive an open, breathing attention that may reveal insight into the associated experience.

For where there is Attention, there is Intention; and where there is intention there is direction, and hence, saturation and healing. When your awareness totally embraces a sensation or condition, that state is absorbed into the union of that attention and there can be resolution. A bridge is built between the observed and the observer. Denial and rejection are replaced by acceptance and inquiry which allows us to unite with ourselves and feel whole, rather than a fragmented, disconnected array of random sensation. This evolving sensibility begins to dissolve any notion of being a 'victim' of past conditioning and is gradually replaced by qualities of strength and self-mastery. As your relationship to the issues alters, so does your perception of yourself.

On more subtle emotional and psychic levels, observing the breath can bring fresh insight into any weaknesses or vulnerability in your energy that may have been caused by accumulated fears or false conditioning. Where you may have gaps in your confidence and faith, where you can fall into shadow and confusion.

As this process develops you are able to let go of 'thinking' you are suffering, as the pain of identification with the form dissolves into your breath, into your greater awareness.

We are no longer focusing on pain or insecurity, we are focused on the breath moving through those feelings. We begin to let go, to surrender to detachment, to fly the white flag. We open with acceptance to love and embrace all those hidden and hurting parts of ourselves. We become one with the process of Becoming. The following Breath Awareness Meditation is to help attune you to the subtle flow of your breathing. This is an effective practice to open the door for your Attention to engage with the passage of your breath as it journeys through your body. Focus lightheartedly on the feeling of your breath, as the breath is subtle. Concentrating too heavily will miss the impulse in your body that breaths. You are *following* the breath, you are not controlling it. Just allow the breath to happen naturally and maintain a soft focus on the sensation of breathing.

This Breath Awareness practice can effectively be incorporated during physical yoga asanas bringing a peaceful mind to your practice. Breath Awareness will enrich the circulation of *prana* and generate a positive, receptive attitude for deepening integration, relaxation and repose.

In times of stress or anxiety, or when you feel emotionally disturbed Breath Awareness Meditation also helps to diffuse the negative symptoms and brings you back into a sense of balance. For those who find it difficult to sit and meditate you can easily lie down to benefit from this practice. Breath Awareness is also an excellent deep relaxation exercise at night that helps the mind unwind and encourages deep sleep.

GUIDANCE FOR AWARENESS MEDITATION

Create a mental *mudra* (*attitude or stance*) of acceptance and inquiry into how your body actually feels in the moment.

Avoid judging your body by thinking 'oh my body is so tight' or 'I am no good at this' and instead just focus on your breathing and accept your body the way it is.

If you criticize yourself and carry on an internal dialogue of judgment and rejection you will only push the resistance further in.

What resists persists! When you accept a feeling or a sensation your mind travels beneath the surface and superficial experience of it, and you get in touch with another dimension of the resistance. Pain is a great teacher.

This acceptant attitude allows the condition to change, often dissolving the tension altogether, as the reason for its existence in the first place maybe due to psychological or emotional tensions that do not actually have any physical limitations. The dynamic lives in the *relationship* between your body and mind not necessarily in the physical form of your body.

BREATH AWARENESS MEDITATION

Place your right hand on your abdomen
And your left hand on your heart
As you breathe in
Feel which hand rises more
If your left hand over the heart
Rises more than right hand
Begin to breathe more deeply
So that your right hand is gently pushed up as you inhale
And falls as you exhale
As your breath begins to regulate itself
Breathing slowly
Bring your Attention to the place within you
That draws the breath in and lets it go
Where the impulse to breathe in originates
Just allow your Awareness to contemplate the feeling
That pulls the breathe in

This drawing in of life energy
And the feeling as you release it
As you exhale
Tune your mind into observing the breath
The expansion of your body as you inhale
Then the softening as you exhale
As you let go of what you do not need
Let your breath lead
And your mind will follow
You are following your breath
Not the breath following you

Allow your breathing to be natural
Free from manipulation or anticipation
Just let it be as it is
Observe the natural rhythm of the breath
How it changes, ebbs and flows
Befriend your breath
Becoming intimate with your breath

Just allow whatever feelings arise within you to be there
Give them space to breathe
Space to relax
Space to change
Embrace them in your breath
Put aside judging your feelings
Or rejecting them
Simply let them be there

Simply being with yourself
Being with your breath
Trusting your breath to flow where it will
Simply Breathing

Meditation, in essence, is a state of fundamental rest.

-Aitkin Roshi, Diamond Sangha, HI

THE DANCE OF
MOVEMENT & STILLNESS

A LITTLE BOGA

BOGA IS THE ANTITHESES OF YOGA in the sense that yoga is a spiritually imbued discipline with rituals of practice and boga represents fun and games, the abandonment of any righteous or spiritual formality, it is the dance of life. I had learnt that to really know how to be a yogini and practice yoga, I needed to learn how to let go of certain inhibitions and self-conscious limitations to help liberate my body from any self-imposed identities. This is quite a Tantric approach. Though, like all forms, boga can also be seen as a spiritual practice when done mindfully.

When Vairocena asked me to go and watch her dance at a club in Seattle Washington DC, I wandered how someone so fresh, vivacious and grounded could possibly become an erotic dancer in the mid-afternoon of a Seattle bar. This was Burlesque in it most personalized form. Yet, there she was, in cowboy boots and Stetson, a halter slung across her naked hips, taking undoubtable pleasure in her own jolly nude performance. Just being herself, her fair skin and almost white blond natural curls bouncing audaciously on her healthy yogic shoulders, without any shadow of a doubt that she was doing the right thing. I was really impressed by her joy more than anything else. Vairocena was one of my close friends and had become a fellow meditator and yogini. Dancing had always been at the very core of my fun and self-expression, I loved rhythm and music of many kinds, and I had danced every night through a few wonderful years in the pulsating cavern of the Melkweg in Amsterdam. I'd also studied Kathak, northern Indian dance in Sante Fe, New Mexico, and had taken on board the discipline of the movement and form, wore chattering bells on my ankles and undertook the strong emphasis on the ritual of performance. Kathak tells stories through dance of the Hindu gods and goddesses and I had learnt some beautiful steps, hand mudras and facial expressions.

Feeling sensual on the dance floor was natural for me, yet actually being able to open myself enough to consciously project that sensuality on a stage, to perform to a captive audience who were *expecting* me to be sexually provocative was a totally new experience, the idea of which sent fire throughout my body and I wanted to try it out. To be able to dance naked very well you require huge confidence and also I feel, qualities of self-love and kindness which you may think is strange. I had always admired the form of the Geisha and temple dancers of India and read many stories of women saints, such as the great Sufi poet Mirabai, who abandoned her modesty and roamed naked in the forest. When told to wear clothes because there were men in sight, she would say "I see no men", to show that she only saw the soul and that she did not identify with the body as either masculine or feminine. I was, undoubtedly, a far cry from being Mirabai and this club was a city bar but in my mind I abandoned the form and entered into the exercise wholeheartedly.

Could I place myself in the cauldron of burning exposure and find my space under the spotlight of erotic dance, actually be a burlesque dancer? I wanted to experience the freedom and beauty of this ancient rite, this exotic intimacy that had been the strength of many women, not only to entertain but to offer homage to the deities in ancient temples. Could I channel that inner connection with my roots, from my first and second chakra, earthy and connected to my third eye, my consciousness? Could I master it and communicate that essence through my body so that it meant something to me, so that it flowed from my consciousness in the same way that I practiced yoga? So that it gave me and my audience a feeling of liberation, of joy, of inner freedom?

Many years ago in Holland, when I had played Nuit the Egyptian goddess of the infinite night sky, in a drama group called Painted Stages and Masked Stages I had tasted this body heat. That play was a mythological drama depicting the story of Ra, the sun god, and the Goddess Nut who I had played and danced fearlessly around the stage. I thought of that time as I contemplated this new attraction to the edge of myself and after years of living in retreat this seemed like a true Boga experiment.

Simply, I would have to be brave, and bravery always takes a certain measure of abandon, of risk. I knew that that is what gives the experience an edge, an energy, a glowing ember that must be delved into in total acceptance of yourself – and a sense of freedom from fear, of total trust. Like falling backwards or walking on hot coals.

This was certainly not for everyone, but I knew it was for me as all my senses were alight at the very thought of such dancing. That rush of blood to the base of my spine and down my legs, to my root charka, my energy was ignited but riddled with fear; with fear of judgment, of rejection, of seeming social moorings and frames of reference that in my intimate inner reality had no true place. Did not really exist. Could I do it! Who would I be then? How would I dance? What would I feel like? Varocena had really just been herself and that was why it worked. She was authentic, in touch with her own unique sensuality yet performing at the same time. A Dakini Yogini Burlesque Dancer.

I saw many women dance that day and each one was different, unique, offering their inner connection to themselves in a myriad of forms. Some were out of work ballerinas who skillfully wrapped their legs around the pole and gracefully moved across the floor like swans and gazelles, seductively doing the splits and piroeting on tip-toe. Others possessed a natural earthy rhythm of movement or bodies oozing with sensual generosity. No-one was the same and hence created a personal message, a signature style like perfume you may like or not. They each had their own expression, their own vibration, their own inner universe to draw from and here was my clue to finding my own creative sensual center of gravity, my own source through which I could perform an intimately provocative dance.

Vairocena and I were part of the same Sufi yoga school, where we practiced Kundalini yoga and Rudra meditation amongst other deep, purifying and transformative practices. We were all burning up the dross, the excess baggage of our accumulated selves, and some of the girls had discovered how liberating and joyful an experience this form of dance could be. Being sensual was in my soul, an essential part of my inner dynamic, my personal chemistry and my connection with life. So, one wet Seattle night Vairocena took me to another club that had a special 'first time' night where girls who had never performed before in this way, could experiment. I saw it as an initiation.

So here I was, having chosen a costume that tried to bridge my spiritual nature with my sensuality. White, all white lace stockings, bra, pearls and bracelets and long elbow length gloves, with silver leather shoes that I tried to keep on by tying white silk ribbons around the sole all the way up my ankles. But, when I got out there I just felt too white... the lights were bright, people were cheering me on and the noise prevented me from really tuning into the music. The audience here was not what I was expecting! I just wanted to run but focused on my feet to keep me grounded, the rhythm of the music and my loyal breath all keeping me balanced. It was a restrained performance to say the least but I knew I could master this, so undeterred I resolved to try again on a regular night when the energy was a little more subdued and I could just blend in.

And so my twelve weeks as a burlesque dancer at Vairocena's club began. The club had an orderly set-up and on any given night there be between 10 and 15 girls dancing. Three individual crescent shaped stages ran along one long wall backed by huge mirrors. Our audience sat at small circular tables in the softly lit crimson interior like a small theatre. Each one of us had to dance on each stage in successive rotation so you might perform 5 times a night on all 3 stages. The center stage was when the music was our choice and the resident DJ had a list of the tracks and girls names in successive order so that when you left the first stage and edged your way up the four wooden steps to the center stage, your favorite track was playing. I had a few favorites like Jimi Hendrix 'White Room', Pink Floyd 'Dark Side of the Moon', ACDC 'House of Cards', Patti Smith 'Horses', Blondie, Eric Burden and The Animals.

This was an utterly unique diverse time and I met some extraordinary people. Dancing burlesque from 9pm to 2am three or four nights a week certainly got me into incredible shape as it was such a total form of exercise. I found that this form of communication allowed me to harness my sexuality and experience where it came from within me and how to channel this raw energy. Sexual energy and creative energy come from the same source and have the power to transform, to alter how one sees and experiences oneself. I began to realize how within this context of movement and gesture I could equally free myself from habitual resistance and tension on a very primary level that reached back to old, even karmic programs of inferiority or shame. This became a tantric exercise of exploring intimacy with myself. Seeing into myself.

Into me see…

My imagination was inspired to create different costumes to embellish the qualities of my inner vibration and deliver performances that were connected to my own expression of burlesque. From elaborate bare footed eastern flavored Dance of the Seven Veils to nothing more than a lame gold bikini with heels, anklets and earrings and combining yoga with dance moves and rhythm. I used my breath, balance and inner vibration to express this intimacy with a growing ease and pleasure that also helped me to integrate a hidden memory of myself as a temple dance in ancient Egypt aeons ago for which I have cellular memories. There was so much fun, pleasure, skill and joy in performing like this and I felt I had passed through some ancient rite of womanhood.

The path of yoga, and of tantra can take many forms, the essential lesson of practice remaining constant in that it is the relationship to the form that creates the outcome, not the form itself. Yet the chosen form carries inherently within it the conditions and boundaries that define it and give it shape and structure. These boundaries ultimately become the tools one learns to perfect the form and then use to go beyond their seeming limitations. The dance, the structure of the form becomes a path, a discipline, and like all disciplines a freedom lies hidden there, a freedom to change. A path of transformation opens up and form becomes formless again, or in the Taoist words of Donovan, *'First there is a mountain, then there is no mountain, then there is.'*

TANTRIC CIRCUIT BREATHING

There are different ways to circulate prana and focus on the chakras you wish to energize, open and enrich. I have found this breath practice to be so effective and dynamic that I share it here by calling it Tantric Circuit Breathing. The purpose of the circuit is to bring fresh conscious prana, vital energy, into the creative sexual chakras and can also be helpful to balance oversexed desire as well as boost sexual energy. The intelligent and conscious circulation of prana re-establishes the optimum balance for your whole being so if out of balance, will restore it. Practice awakens the flow of your creative sexual energy, and you may feel more in touch with your inner 'source' and others will feel more in touch with the 'source' as it lives in you. This is only the beginning practice as you will naturally want to bring that flow of breath up to the heart charka, and the second practice given here addresses this balance.

TANTRIC CIRCUIT BREATHING PRACTICE

Be aware of the soles of your feet
and breathe into them as if you were
pulling the energy of breath in through the soles of your feet.
Breathe all the way up your legs to your yoni or lingham
imagining the energy crossing over at the base of your spine.
As you exhale feel the breath
going back down the legs to the feet
then concentrate on your feet for a while
until you need to breathe in again.
Repeat this circulatory breath about 12 times
Letting the breath flow easily paying
particular attention to soles of your feet.

DOUBLE BREATHS

Double Breaths link your Heart and Hara with the
Crown of the head. These are your second navel and
root chakra Muladhara and Svadhisthana, with the
fourth Heart Chakra Ajna and the seventh Chakra
above the crow of your head Sahasrara. Practicing this
breath will connect up all these vital energy centers
bringing a revived flow of prana to their circuit. The
purpose is to strengthen the relationship between your
creative, sexual centers in the root chakras with the
empathetic and compassionate qualities of love in your

heart. The heart will then serve to purify the magnetism of raw deep orange energy of the lower chakras. That flow of energy is then channeled up through the light of the crown chakra where the gateway to the divine is located. This is also an avenue of pure life force that encourages release of tensions or restrictions and brings a sense of spiritual consciousness to your experience, either alone or with another person.

DOUBLE BREATHS PRACTICE

Breathe deeply into the heart and upper lung
holding the breath there for a few seconds
gently pushing your shoulders back
Then exhale half of the breath
and directly inhale again
all the way into your abdomen
holding the breath there for another few seconds
Now slowly exhale
visualizing the breath flowing through the crown of
your head like a fountain above you
.....way above your head
roll your eyes up under closed eye lids
looking upwards and inwards to the center of your forehead
where your attention naturally gathers
as the breath flows out through the crown of your head
imagine it falling back down all around you
to your feet

then just bathe in that experience
just observe how you feel without trying
to change it

You can do up to 3 or 4 breaths at a time, pausing after each breath to fully experience and integrate the shifts in energy. It's a joy...

Yoga practice teaches us the dance of movement and stillness. Movement magnifies the nourishing elements within stillness, and stillness defines the purpose of movement. Hatha Yoga means *ha* sun and *tha* moon. This can be interpreted as the male and female aspects of practice. Movement is the Sun nature of yoga and can be seen as the male *Assertive* outgoing side of ourselves that heats up and regenerates energy. Stillness is the Moon nature of yoga, the feminine *Receptive* reflective side of ourselves that cools down, contains and preserves energy. Hatha also represents the in and out vibration and flow of the breath. As the body breathes in it lifts and makes a subtle Ha sound. When we exhale the body makes a soft Tha sound as the breath leaves the body.

The play and dance between movement and stillness is an ongoing phenomenon of human life. When we move, the world about us also moves, altering our perceptions and thereby influencing our relationship with all aspects of life. Each one of us may be looking at the same scene yet we all see something different as each of us is physically and mentally poised in a different position. The rhythm of life evolves into times of rest, when stillness enriches observation, digestion, integration and growth. A seed planted within the earth's surface needs to be left alone, quiet and undisturbed in order for it to reach its full potential. Deep sleep in children is the fertile environment for maximum growth and for all of us to recoup, heal and recharge. Hibernation and Retreat are all based on this need we have to restore balance. Stillness also engenders qualities of nurture, acceptance, reflection and ultimately, profound change.

Yoga is by nature a transformative process that utilizes and influences the relationship between your body and all its functions. Within the practice of yoga it is your *awareness* of the process of going into an asana (posture) that decides how deeply the movement will internally change the posturing of your inner state of body and being. Your undivided attention brings you into the experience of unity with the body and mind thereby dissolving inner conflicts and feelings of separation or disassociation. Disassociation is not the same as detachment. Detachment implies that there is awareness and sensitivity to an experience yet you are objective and not identified with it. You are in an observing frame of mind. Disassociation means that there is an unwillingness to feel or acknowledge the existence of a sensation even though it is there within you. Being numb, ignoring or refusing to allow the reality of a sensation or experience to be recognized is disassociation. Many feelings of stress and tension are caused by the inability to focus your mind where you actually are *in the moment* and accept what is there. The mind likes to wander here and there which diffuses our attention and energy levels. Many forms of western exercise ignore the intervention of the mind and the benevolent part it can play within the power of movement. Yoga is the reverse and requires our full presence of mind to realize the benefits of practice.

The postures themselves take on a new meaning and significance when your mind is applied. When you breathe into the physical sensations of resistance or tensions, you bring consciousness and prana into those places. This naturally helps to liberate the blocked energy submerged there. The flow of prana is directed by your consciousness and generates the depth and power of prana.

In the same way your experience of stillness, of the integration of movement is indicative of your inner focus and breathing patterns. Whilst holding a posture, breathe into all those parts of yourself that feel restricted or tight. When you breathe out, toxicity, tension and old psychic matter is also eliminated, as your mind lets go of the need for struggle. As you physically extend yourself the mind stretches too, and the relaxation process begins to unfold. Your body may be tense but your mind can be free. Avoid identifying with the struggle in your body and just calmly observe it, breathing as freely as you can with an acceptant attitude. Detach yet do not disassociate.

METTA BHAVANA
The Sea Of Love

LOVING KINDNESS MEDITATION

Whilst present at a Wembley conference for the Dalai Lama someone asked him whether he thought Buddhism was the best religion. In response the Dalai Lama replied, 'Buddhism is best for me. My religion is kindness.'

This clear and compassionate response dissolved any comparison or duality in the mind of the questioner and we all witnessed the unmistakable generosity with which the Dalai Lama had responded.

Metta is the cultivation of Loving Kindness. It re-teaches us the inner language of love, the speaking of which generates Compassion, Sympathetic Joy and Equanimity.

Metta is the Sea of Love that ebbs and flows without ceasing within the heart of mankind. It resides within the natural desire to make peace with ourselves, to make peace with our friends, our families with all of life. Simply to make Peace.

This is not complicated. Though perhaps hidden, we know already the feeling and flavor of Peace and that is why we seek it ...... because we know that peace is already here. We know this genetically, as part of our chemical makeup and intuitively, as part of our spiritual heritage as Human Beings. We do not bully peace out of ourselves. We need to find a gentle way to tend that pool of bliss so that we can reside there and Be Peace. Peace is a part of who we are.

We are all born with the potential, the capacity to be at peace, to be loving and receptive. Yet somehow we have lost touch, forgotten the intimacy of inner peace. We have accumulated an excess of impressions, of sensations, of thoughts and images which cloud the view and numb our senses, cluttering the mind. Peace is hidden there, waiting to be uncovered, to be recognized. Waiting to be Called. Peace is our inner sanctuary, it is our first home.

As in all things, peace is an energy that vibrates and responds. It does not exist in isolation but as a communicating vibration that influences our relationship to all things. It is a way of communicating. Peace is a force for healing, an all-encompassing presence that accepts and surrenders with grace. Peace is the true power of our Human Spirit that overcomes hardship and pain and has faith in its own nature. It is as much a means as it is an end.   In the words of Mahatma Gandhi *The process and the goal are not separate, they are one.'*

We know what peace is not. It is not war, or strife, or greed or anger. Neither is it fear, jealousy or resentment. Peace does not exist in cruelty, in the fight for being right or the struggle for superiority.

We need to call peace by its true names so that it can emerge from a place of intimacy into the fullness of our conscious awareness. We need to speak the language of peace in order to make friends with ourselves, with our lives. And there is a language for peace that cultivates its presence and strengthens its reality in our lives. It is this language, this dialogue which Metta teaches us to contemplate and understand.

THE DISCIPLINE OF ZAZEN and the definitive practice of Vipassana had graciously opened the mind, yet too had ripened the fruit of my heart to the richly laden taste of Metta Bhavana. I was truly blessed to have been initiated into this heavenly practice by Anagarika Munidra on that first ten day Vipassana retreat in Maui, and later by the Sharon Salzburg during the silent three month retreat in Barre, Massachusetts at The Insight Mediation Society. Those first sessions were like drinking from a flacon of the finest wine that allowed the depth of my feelings and emotions to roll sweetly through me and be experienced as a divine maternal embrace.

In the years that followed, sitting in the airy rafters of my Maui Haiku home, a two story hut perched on the edge of a Eucalyptus grove that looked out to sea, I would bask in the fragrance of Metta each morning for two timeless, god given hours. The luxury of this space, the wealth of this gift to the heart, saturated a longing I could not have realized until it was tasted. This meditation was like receiving a perfect bouquet of glorious lilies and gardenias every day that filled my world with a fragrance so intoxicating I was completely addicted. The more I practiced the richer became the soil of my awareness deepening the divine peace I felt with all beings everywhere. A priceless treasure by simply siting on my zafu.

Metta Bhavana means Loving Kindness and originates from the Theravadan tradition of Buddhism which is the oldest known form of Buddhist practice and literally means The Teachings of the Elders. Within the great teachings of Vipassana (Insight Meditation) the infinite compassion of Buddha realized that the human heart requires direct conversation and guidance in the art of healing in order to completely liberate the mind. Metta Bhavana meditation concentrates on enriching the qualities of *Acceptance, Gratitude and Forgiveness* as the key attributes that dissolve blockages in the realms of our emotional freedom, often caused by feelings of regret, remorse, resentment, guilt and blame.

This heavenly practice is literally at the very heart of human freedom and enlightenment and I recommend that all those who seek to resolve conflict of any nature, give themselves unreservedly to this transforming experience. You will be rewarded with the sweetest nectar you could imagine.

CULTIVATING JOY & COMPASSION

We are all born with the potential, the capacity to be at peace yet somehow we have lost touch with and forgotten the intimacy of inner peace even though peace is a natural part of who you already are. We have accumulated an excess of impressions, sensations, experiences and conditioned responses that cloud the mind and heart and numb our innate sensitivity. Yet Peace is hidden deep there, waiting to be re-discovered and recognized. Peace is our own inner sanctuary and our first home. Peace is the true power of the human spirit that overcomes hardship and pain and has faith in its own nature. It is as much a means as it is an end.

We know what peace is not. It is not war, or strife, or greed or anger. Neither is it fear, jealousy or resentment. Peace does not exist in cruelty, in the fight for being right or the struggle for superiority. We need to call peace up within us into the fullness of our conscious awareness. Creating peace is making friends with ourselves and with our lives. We need to speak the language of peace so that we cultivate its presence in reality of life.

The road to cultivating your peace begins with developing compassion for yourself and this path has been exquisitely formed into the practice of Metta Bhavana Meditation. Metta is a Pali word which means Loving Kindness, friendship or simply kindness and is an ancient Buddhist practice whose principles can be seen as the bedrock to many spiritual traditions and religious doctrines. If you have a religion or spiritual practice that you follow, this meditation will in no way deter you from it or clash with other doctrines. Metta is a pure practice that supports you, whatever your spiritual beliefs.

The joys of Metta reach us in ways you could not have imagined, as though you have drunk long and deep from the soul of life itself that softens and nurtures your innermost being. Metta is a balm for healing the human heart.

THE FOUR PRINCIPLES OF METTA BHAVANA

1. ### ACCEPTANCE

    The benefits of cultivating qualities of acceptance dissolves criticism, judgement, jealousy, loss, anger, emotional and physical pain, feelings of separation or isolation and create empathy, sympathy, deep relaxation and joy.

    This principle of Acceptance is an important theme within body work therapy as shown within this handbook. Acceptance becomes the therapists' invisible aid during therapy, who you bring to life through integrating the guidance given in the chapters Your Breath and Your Mind. Acceptance creates stillness and a space for change.

2. ### GRATITUDE

    The benefits of cultivating feelings of gratitude dissolve craving, greed, grasping, frustration, selfishness and dissatisfaction and create qualities of appreciation, thankfulness, generosity and equanimity.

    Unless you can appreciate your own body, your health, your sanity, your family, your friends, your abilities, your home and all the many riches within and around you, you will never be satisfied. By being thankful for who you are and what you have, more will be given in body, mind and spirit. Gratitude brings joy to the heart. Count your blessings.

3. FORGIVENESS

The benefits of generating qualities of forgiveness dissolve feelings of blame, guilt, sadness, grief, remorse and regret and create a powerful sense of inner freedom, healing, reconciliation and compassion.

Forgiveness can be a slow yet deeply healing process which does not mean that you condone whatever has occurred in the past. Neither does it mean that you forget any injustice that may have wounded you in any way. Forgiveness frees you from reliving the suffering caused by the continued feelings of grief or blame or regret in the present.

Forgiveness is a force for reconciliation beyond the reasoning of the mind, allowing you to feel liberated and healed at the very heart of the matter.

THE FOUR HINDRANCES TO PEACE AND HAPPINESS

REGRET causes us to hold on and live in the past.

BLAME blocks true forgiveness.

GUILT is how we punish ourselves.

ANGER is hidden or suppressed hurt.

Clearing the mind and heart of these negative elements makes space to plant new and positive seeds to nourish and fulfill your life's potential.

4. LOVING KINDNESS

The benefits of creating qualities of loving kindness dissolve feelings of struggle, strife, inadequacy and vulnerability, generating feelings of strength, protection, contentment, kindness and nurture.

In this world of diversity, where we can experience and witness the blessings of wealth, peace and wisdom, and the hardships of poverty, injustice, sickness and war a compassionate mind and heart is a simple act of human kindness. Reflect on those that have been charitable to you and how you can be kind and generous also. Kindness is its own reward.

How far you go in life depends on your being tender with the young, compassionate with the aged, sympathetic with the striving, and tolerant of the weak and the strong. Because someday you will have been all of these.

-George Washington
-Carver

THE PRACTICE OF METTA

METTA MEDITATION PRACTICE is a simple process of sitting quietly and repeating specific phrases that relate to these principles, slowly and silently within the sanctity of your own mind and heart. You can create your own language of Metta in the way that your thoughts naturally flow if you chose. Here Metta is presented in its traditional form which carries with it the blessings and energy of all those who have practiced in exactly this way since Buddha gave us this great teaching 2000 years ago.

The practice can be focused on to extend out to other people in your life and throughout the world in a more global context. The fundamental purpose of Metta is to purify, nurture and heal yourself, the benefits of which will extend out to all whose lives you touch.

PREPARATION

Begin with Breath Awareness Meditation to enable you to focus as clearly as possible.

Softly close your eyes, relax your face, inwardly smiling.

Be aware of your posture, alignment and presence.

Practice slowly repeating each phrase of each of the four attributes at least six times then flow to the next.

Allow your breath to help you relax into the beauty of this meditation.

ACCEPTANCE

Saying peacefully to yourself

'As I am, may I completely accept myself. I completely accept myself'

Allow qualities of acceptance to flow through you.

Relax into yourself, completely accepting how you feel

If resistant or contrary feelings arise, breathe into them

And accept them also.

Repeating slowly with each breath

'As I am I completely accept myself.

I completely accept myself'

GRATITUDE

Saying peacefully to yourself

'May I be thankful for all that has been given. May I be thankful'.

Bring to mind all that you are and all that you have.

Allow feelings of appreciation and thankfulness to flow through you.

If negative or contrary feelings arise, breathe into them, relax and let them go.

Repeating slowly in your mind

'May I be thankful for all that has been given. May I am thankful'.

FORGIVENESS OF SELF

Saying peacefully to yourself

"May I forgive myself for any harm I have caused myself or any other being. May I be forgiven"'

As you peacefully repeat the phrase allow any feelings of guilt, regret or remorse to come to the surface of your mind and heart.

Let feelings of forgiveness come to you, letting go of stress and relaxing.

Receiving feelings of forgiveness.

Repeating slowly in your mind

"May I forgive myself for any harm I have caused myself or any other being. May I be forgiven"'

FORGIVENESS OF OTHERS

Forgiveness of others can be a far more challenging practice yes this will allow you to experience the true nature of reconciliation which is one of the most powerful and transformative elements of self-healing. This first meditation for forgiveness of others can deepen self-healing, relaxing your heart on visceral and subtle levels, giving health benefits within so many elements   However, if there is someone in particular that you wish to forgive The Seed of Light Visualization offered below will help you pave the way from your heart to theirs.

THE PRACTICE

Saying peacefully to yourself

"May I forgive any being who has ever harmed me.
May I forgive."

Let qualities of forgiveness flow out of you, relaxing into your body and breath. If feelings of blame or anger arise, breathe into them, relaxing into yourself.

Repeating slowly in your mind and heart

"May I forgive any being who has ever harmed me.
May I forgive."

FORGIVENESS OF A SPECIFIC PERSON
With Seed of Light Visualization

This is to be practiced when forgiving a specific person whose name you may or may not know.

THE PRACTICE

Imagine that you plant a seed of light within your heart.

Bring to mind the person you wish to forgive, seeing them in your mind's eye.

From the seed of light within you build a bridge of light from your heart to theirs.

Plant a seed of light in their heart and practice the following Metta.

Saying peacefully to yourself: *"May I forgive you for any harm you have caused me. May I forgive you."*

This can bring up intense feelings of resentment, fear or anger. Breathe into these feelings focusing on the bridge of light from the seed in your heart to theirs. Breathe into that bridge.

Repeat the words slowly in your mind and in your heart.

"May I forgive you for any harm you have caused me. May I forgive you."

Loving Kindness Practice

This is the sealing element of a Metta Bhavana practice that brings qualities of kindness and joy towards yourself and others. Repeating the phrase slowly with a true sense of the meaning of the words flowing through you.

Saying peacefully:

"May I be happy
May I be peaceful
May I be free from suffering
As I am, may all beings be free"

Universal Loving Kindness

Here we include all people and beings everywhere beginning with those who are in the forefront of your mind. Visualize your dear family, friends, work colleagues, those who come to your mind through distant association and so on.

Saying peacefully

"May you be happy
May you be peaceful
May you be free
As I am, may all beings be free"

Then move your attention outwards to all the people in your house, your street and peacefully repeat the phrase.

Gradually visualize your neighborhood, your town or city, all the people, trees, flowers, animals and birds there. Repeating the phrase over and over.

Move your mind into the country side and into your whole country. Visualize other countries and all the life within them and repeat the phrase.

Think of the all the oceans, the islands, the forests, the high mountains, rivers and wildlife there. Repeating the phrase.

Expand your mind and heart even further and visualize the skies, space, the sun, the moon and all the stars and planets. Repeating the phrase.

"May you be happy
May you be peaceful
May you be free
As I am, may all beings be free"

In that expanded all-embracing state of consciousness simple meditate, be still in that vastness for a while.

Then breathe deeply, consciously, bring your hands into Prayer Mudra or touch your forehead to the floor, the earth.

Be aware of your body, your own earthly presence

Vipassana and Metta originate from the Theravadin tradition of Buddhist practice. Vipassana means 'Insight' and reflects the male, yang aspect of our nature. It is investigative, inquiring and assertive, yet contains within it a foundation of receptivity. A foundation of acceptance that supports the natural arising of our neurosis. By this I mean, the constant ongoing 'interpretation' in our minds of the ceaseless changing phenomena unfolding within and around us.

Metta is the feminine aspect of our perception, of our essential nature. It is the all-embracing, all forgiving conscious compassion of the heart. The omnipresence of forgiveness and acceptance. The consciousness of Metta embraces all with the acknowledgment of choice to act from the heart. Metta and Vipassana are two sides of the same coin. They exist side by side, one supporting the other, living within each other's elements like the yin-yang symbol of light and dark. The seed of one aspect lives in the omnipresence of the other. They are one process.

Both aspects are deeply compassionate. Metta activates the trust of letting-go, the flow of love within and through the heart. This naturally generates the release of deep waters within us, melted through the warmth of compassion. Areas of frozen feeling are dissolved in the fire of creative, unconditional love. Of sympathetic joy. Tears can flow as the language of our hearts washing our wounds, our pain our forgetfulness in a sea of love.

Only what is true remains. All that is false, that can no longer uphold itself in the cauldron of our growing surrender and inquiry, dissolves. What is left is the pure fruition of our journey that teaches freedom from suffering. Metta is the cultivation of compassion, the mother of healing. The one who acknowledges the pain and applies the medicine.

THE RAISING OF THE OX

As a child I found myself continually experimenting with the sense of presence and awareness, like a game of being or not being. Or, *'Am I or am I not'*. I can remember clearly walking up the stairs at home, at perhaps the age of seven or eight and spontaneously stopping and thinking *'Here I am right now, I am walking up these stairs, I am breathing, I can feel my body here, I will never forget this moment, I am."* And I never have. The stance I held, that spontaneous moment of intense awareness, every detail of the staircase, all served to anchor me in the reality of that moment, in my presence, in life unfolding right then and there. Feeling as though I was somehow observing myself from above or was it from deep within? I didn't know but wanted to be sure I really was here, alive, in this body. And now I realize that nothing has changed. That same impetus to completely unite with the moment remains, has evolved, has weaved itself like a golden thread of consciousness through this life. Bringing a sense of happiness and connection to all things.

At night, before sleeping, I would often cry to my mother asking her how I could know that I would wake up again if I fell asleep. I wanted to know where 'I' went when sleeping and said I was afraid to die in my sleep and not *know* I had died. My mother laughed, telling me not to worry, and that I would not die in my sleep. I know now that I did not want to die unconsciously; that did worry me.

Many years later when looking through the library at the Insight Meditation Society in Massachusetts I found a book on the Bodhicitta - the cultivation of the mind of a Bodhisattva. In this book the very first spiritual practice given is to contemplate the dying of your physical body as you go to sleep as a way of deepening your consciousness. I felt a tremendous rush of energy as the memory of those childhood fears suddenly arose. I had not thought about my worrisome nights as a child and the practices that had spontaneously arisen until that moment.

Within the dialogue of Zen teachings there is a phrase called *The Raising of the Ox*. This saying points to the realization that once you have conceived of the thought or experienced a state of awareness that embraces, yet transcends all thought and sensation you will *always seek to* know this, to become this. To be enlightened. There is no turning back. Once you have been immersed in this boundless, limitless consciousness that is truly detached from habitual conditioning, yet aware and sensitive to all that is, the trace of this awareness will never leave you. When Gautama Buddha sat with Acolytes in the forest he would ask them whether they really wanted to begin the path of liberation, because once begun it would gnaw away at their being, at their hearts and minds until they gave it their full attention; until complete authenticity had been revealed... your true nature...your Buddha nature.

Recalling this story is an expression of gratitude and awe for the persistence of this stubborn patient Ox who arose to become the undying faithful nature, guide and anchor within this mysterious life.

PRAISE FOR THE BOOK

"It's always touching and transformative to learn from personal stories and teachings. Jacqueline's insightful reflections resonate with the inner journeys of a generation of liberated women who have freed themselves from restricted perspectives of how to live and love, and found their own truth and happiness through timeless wisdom"

Dr. Harbeen Arora,
ALL Ladies League (ALL) &
Women Economic Forum (WEF)

ABOUT THE AUTHOR

Jacqualine is a qualified yoga and meditation teacher with traditional roots and a global wealth of knowledge and experience enriching her life and career. Founder of Evolve Healing Arts School of body mind therapies and Yogic Solutions she leads training programs in many modalities operating as a Wellness Spa Consultant and Director. She has studied, lived and worked extensively in the USA, Hawaii, India, China, Japan, Bhutan, Thailand, Spain, Italy, Mauritius, Seychelles and the UK. A published author and audio artist she became dedicated to creating innovative signature spa rituals and products 20 years ago and continues to evolve her vocation.

Printed in Great Britain
by Amazon

42084484R00111